FIVE LATE
ROMANTIC POETS

THE POETRY BOOKSHELF

General Editor: James Reeves

Robert Graves: *English and Scottish Ballads*
Tom Scott: *Late Medieval Scots Poetry*
James Reeves: *Chaucer: Lyric and Allegory*
William Tydeman: *English Poetry 1400–1580*
Martin Seymour-Smith: *Shakespeare's Sonnets*
Martin Seymour-Smith: *Longer Elizabethan Poems*
James Reeves: *John Donne*
Maurice Hussey: *Jonson and the Cavaliers*
Jack Dalglish: *Eight Metaphysical Poets*
James Reeves and Martin Seymour-Smith: *Andrew Marvell*
Dennis Burden: *Shorter Poems of John Milton*
V. de S. Pinto: *Poetry of the Restoration*
Roger Sharrock: *John Dryden*
James Reeves: *Jonathan Swift*
John Heath-Stubbs: *Alexander Pope*
Francis Venables: *The Early Augustans*
Donald Davie: *The Late Augustans*
Donald Davie: *Augustan Lyric*
F. W. Bateson: *William Blake*
G. S. Fraser: *Robert Burns*
Roger Sharrock: *William Wordsworth*
James Reeves: *S. T. Coleridge*
Robin Skelton: *Lord Byron*
John Holloway: *P. B. Shelley*
James Reeves: *John Clare*
Robert Gittings: *Poems and Letters of John Keats*
Edmund Blunden: *Alfred Lord Tennyson*
James Reeves: *Robert Browning*
James Reeves: *Thomas Gray*
Denys Thompson: *Poetry and Prose of Matthew Arnold*
James Reeves: *Emily Dickinson*
James Reeves: *G. M. Hopkins*
David Wright: *Seven Victorian Poets*
James Reeves: *The Modern Poets' World*
James Reeves: *D. H. Lawrence*
James Reeves: *Five Late Romantic Poets*

EMILY BRONTË
(Artist unknown)

FIVE LATE
ROMANTIC POETS

GEORGE DARLEY
HARTLEY COLERIDGE
THOMAS HOOD
THOMAS LOVELL BEDDOES
EMILY BRONTË

Edited with an Introduction and Commentary

by

JAMES REEVES

HEINEMANN
LONDON

Heinemann Educational Books Ltd

LONDON EDINBURGH MELBOURNE AUCKLAND TORONTO
HONG KONG SINGAPORE KUALA LUMPUR
IBADAN NAIROBI JOHANNESBURG
LUSAKA NEW DELHI

Distributed in the U.S.A. 1974 by
HARPER & ROW PUBLISHERS, INC.
BARNES & NOBLE IMPORT DIVISION
ISBN 06-495819-1
ISBN 0 435 15073 1 (cased)
ISBN 0 435 15074 X (paper)

INTRODUCTION AND NOTES
© JAMES REEVES 1974

FIRST PUBLISHED 1974

Ref PR
1221
F58
cop.1

Published by
Heinemann Educational Books Ltd
48 Charles Street, London W1X 8AH
Printed in Great Britain by Morrison and Gibb Ltd
London and Edinburgh

CONTENTS

HARTLEY COLERIDGE (1796–1849)—*Continued*

THOMAS HOOD (1799–1845)

THOMAS LOVELL BEDDOES (1803–1849)

EMILY BRONTË (1818–1848)

COMMENTARY AND NOTES

PREFACE

In this series, begun over twenty years ago, separate volumes are devoted to the work of the principal poets, anthology volumes to that of significant minors. Every reader knows that much good and interesting poetry is to be found outside the work of major writers. When we speak of the Elizabethan lyric, the Metaphysicals or the Augustans, we include work of this kind. We think of a sort of collective Elizabethan lyrist. When we speak of the Romantics, however, we are thinking chiefly of Blake, Wordsworth, Coleridge and Clare, Shelley, Byron and Keats. We do not normally speak much of minor Romantics. There is no collective Romantic poet; there is no 'school' of Romantic poetry. There are a few major poets, but the minor verse of the period gives no coherent impression of any significance. Romanticism in a sense represents fragmentation, a concentration of interest on great individuals with little in common. The minor poetry of the period—the occasional poems and the album verses—that which occupied the anthologies of the period, is of little interest today and ill repays research. Yet there is significant minor poetry of the early nineteenth century; there are poets worthy of attention. It is the purpose of this volume to represent the best of this poetry.

The five poets here chosen do not form a school, and any general introduction to their work would have little relevance. Instead, a short biographical and critical introduction to each of the five is given.

Are there, then, no similarities and correspondences to be discovered among the best minor poets from Darley to Emily Brontë? The most obvious factor is that all died comparatively young. None lived long after his fiftieth year. All suffered from ill health or material privation or both. As poets these five were in a sense unfulfilled. But they were no mere occasional poets. They were dedicated, and they had something to say. Darley was an articulate critic of current poetic fashions and strove to offer something original. Beddoes cultivated an individual and private sensibility at variance with the currents of his time. Hartley Coleridge, conscious of writing in the shadow of his father and of Wordsworth, also had his personal contribution to make, his own sensibility to explore. His positive achievement, slender as it was and still undervalued, lifts him above the common run of early nineteenth-century poetry. The same may be said of Emily Brontë, as a poet indubitably 'minor' (her greatest poem is in the form of a novel) but, at her best, worthy of as much attention as a good deal of the poetry of the illustrious Victorians who were beginning to attract public notice in her lifetime.

These four cultivated their own private sensibilities and inhabited their own worlds of feeling and imagination. Hood alone is concerned with the society about him.

Other early nineteenth-century strains to be found in these five poets, though not in all alike, are the influence of the Gothic, the obsession with death, the sense of personal isolation and unfulfilment, discontent with current poetic fashions and, finally, an interest in religion. There is even a pre-echo of the near-hysterical evangelism of later times.

Not very much helpful criticism has been written about these poets, but one exception must be acknowledged by anyone trying to get beneath the surface of the minor poetry of the period. This is John Heath-Stubbs' *The Darkling Plain*, the work of a poet with a sympathetic and imaginative insight into the poets he discusses. I am glad to acknowledge my indebtedness to this exceptional book.

For valuable help in the preparation of this volume I am indebted to Stephen Coote and Martin Ryle.

J. R.

Lewes, 1974

SELECT BIBLIOGRAPHY

GEORGE DARLEY

Complete Poetical Works, ed. Ramsay Colles, London 1908.
The Life and Letters of George Darley, C. C. Abbott, 1928.
Votive Tablets, Edmund Blunden, London 1931.
The Darkling Plain, John Heath-Stubbs, London 1950.
Collected Essays V, Robert Bridges, 1931.

HARTLEY COLERIDGE

Letters of Hartley Coleridge, ed. G. E. and E. L. Griggs, 1937.
New Poems, ed. E. L. Griggs, 1942.
Hartley Coleridge: His Life and Work, E. L. Griggs, 1929.
Complete Poetical Works of Hartley Coleridge, ed. R. Colles, Muses'
    Library 1908.

THOMAS HOOD

Poems, ed. C. Dyment, London 1948.
Selected Poems, ed. N. Clubbe, Oxford University Press 1970.
The Darkling Plain, John Heath-Stubbs, London 1950.
Thomas Hood, J. C. Reid, London 1953.
Thomas Hood, L. Brander, British Council, London 1963.

THOMAS LOVELL BEDDOES

Works of T. L. Beddoes, ed. H. W. Donner, Muses' Library 1935.
Thomas Lovell Beddoes: The Making of a Poet, H. W. Donner, 1935.
The Darkling Plain, John Heath-Stubbs, 1950.

The Complete Poems of Emily Jane Brontë, ed. C. W. Hatfield, Oxford University Press 1941.

Emily Brontë: A Critical and Biographical Study, John Hewish, London 1969.

Emily Brontë, Winifred Gérin, Oxford 1971.

GEORGE DARLEY

from *Nepenthe*

O blest unfabled Incense Tree,
That burns in glorious Araby,
With red scent chalicing the air,
Till earth-life grow Elysian there!

Half buried to her flaming breast   5
In this bright tree, she makes her nest,
Hundred-sunned Phœnix! when she must
Crumble at length to hoary dust!

Her gorgeous death-bed! her rich pyre
Burnt up with aromatic fire!   10
Her urn, sight high from spoiler men!
Her birthplace when self-born again!

The mountainless green wilds among,
Here ends she her unechoing song!
With amber tears and odorous sighs   15
Mourned by the desert where she dies!

Laid like the young fawn mossily
In sun-green vales of Araby,
I woke hard by the Phœnix tree
That with shadeless boughs flamed over me,   20
And upward called by a dumb cry
With moonbroad orbs of wonder, I
Beheld the immortal Bird on high
Glassing the great sun in her eye.

Stedfast she gazed upon his fire, 25
Still her destroyer and her sire!
As if to his her soul of flame
Had flown already, whence it came;

Like those that sit and glare so still,
Intense with their death struggle, till 30
We touch, and curdle at their chill!—
But breathing, yet while she doth burn,
    The deathless Daughter of the sun!
Slowly to crimson embers turn
    The beauties of the brightsome one. 35
O'er the broad nest her silver wings
Shook down their wasteful glitterings;
Her brinded neck high-arched in air
Like a small rainbow faded there;
But brighter glowed her plumy crown 40
Mouldering to golden ashes down;
With fume of sweet woods, to the skies,
Pure as a Saint's adoring sighs,
Warm as a prayer in Paradise,
Her life-breath rose in sacrifice! 45
The while with shrill triumphant tone
Sounding aloud, aloft, alone,
Ceaseless her joyful deathwail she
Sang to departing Araby!
    Deep melancholy wonder drew 50
Tears from my heartspring at that view.
Like cresset shedding its last flare
Upon some wistful mariner,
The Bird, fast blending with the sky,
Turned on me her dead-gazing eye 55
Once—and as surge to shallow spray
Sank down to vapoury dust away!

2

Goalward at length untired I flee
Past the still Verdurous Isles, that be
Oases of the herbless sea,   60
And those Happy Gardens placed
Edenlike in an azure waste,
Befanned with sunniest winds, the air
Swims visible in bright halo there,
Feeding with such rich juice the mould   65
That every fruit-tree drops with gold,
In tawny Harvest's pendant ear
Glitters the gold grain twice a year,
Each rivulet doth his bed emboss
With the crisp ore and yellowing dross,   70
His margin trim with asphodel
Gorgeously *flounc'd*; and spreads as well
Woodland wide-over this rich flower
Till each fair Isle thro' dale and fell
Seems to inlap a golden shower   75
Heaven-loved; and where the breezes run
Her wavy grasses full of sun
Flow like a bright flood all in one.
Ah me! how long my soul beguiles
The Siren of those Fortunate Isles!   80

Not less than magic breath had blown
Ashy ambition now to flame,
Within me; but like veins in stone
Red grew the blood in my cold frame:
Tho' drained this life-spring to the lees   85
On lancing rocks—this body worn,
Weed-wrung, and saturate with seas
Gulped thro'—by their wild mercy borne
Half jellied hither, and well-nigh
Piecemeal by those white coursers torn   90
That shook their manes of me, foam high,

3

Cast on their saviour backs forlorn—
Tho' thus my flesh, my spirit still
Is unsubdued! aspiring will
Buoys up my sinking power. 'Tis thine,   95
This quenchless spark! To thee this glow,
This rise from my sea-grave I owe,
Nepenthe! vital fire divine!
Yet ah! what boots, if cup of bliss
Have such a bitter dreg as this?   100
Fragile and faint must I still on
The arduous path that I have gone,
Or burn in my own sighs! Like thee,
A winged cap, O Mercury!
I wear, that lifts me still to heaven,   105
Tho' down to herd with mortals driven.

The Demon's Cave

A shadowy dell, from whence arise
Fen-pamper'd clouds that blot the skies,
And from their sooty bosoms pour
A blue and pestilential shower.
High in the midst a crag-built dome   5
Ruder than Cyclops' mountain-home,
Or that the blood-born giants piled
When Earth was with their steps defiled.
Lightning has scorch'd and blasted all
Within this dark cavernous hall;   10
Through every cranny screams a blast
As it would cleave the rocks at last;
Loud-rapping hail spins where it strikes,
And rain runs off the roof in dykes,

And crackling flame and feathery sleet   15
Hiss in dire contest as they meet;
Tempests are heard to yell around
And inward thunders lift the ground.
   In front a dismal tomb-like throne,
Which Horror scarce would sit upon,   20
Yet on the throne doth sit a thing
In apish state, misnamed a king;
A ghastlier Death, a skeleton,
Not of a man, but a baboon.
His robe a pall, his crown a skull   25
With teeth for gems and grinning full;
His rod of power in his hand,
A serpent writhing round a wand;
With this he tames the gnashing fiends,
Soul-purchased to assist his ends;   30
Yet still they spit and mouth and pierce
If not with fangs with eyes as fierce
Each other—while behind they seek
Their sly revenge and hate to wreak.

O May, thou art a merry time

O May, thou art a merry time,
   Sing hi! the hawthorn pink and pale!
When hedge-pipes they begin to chime,
   And summer-flowers to sow the dale.

When lasses and their lovers meet   5
   Beneath the early village thorn,
And to the sound of tabor sweet
   Bid welcome to the maying morn!

When gray-beards and their gossips come
    With crutch in hand our sports to see,   10
And both go tottering, tattling home,
    Topful of wine as well as glee!

But Youth was aye the time for bliss,
    So taste it, shepherds, while ye may;
For who can tell that joy like this   15
    Will come another holiday?

O May, thou art a merry time,
    Sing hi! the hawthorn pink and pale!
When hedge-pipes they begin to chime,
    And summer-flowers to sow the dale.   20

Noon in the Forest

Deep in a wild sequester'd nook,
Where Phœbus casts no scorching look,
But Earth's soft carpet moist and green
Freckled with golden spots is seen;
Where with the wind that swayeth him   5
The pine spins slowly round his stem;
The willow weeps as in despair
Amid her green dishevelled hair;
And long-arm'd elms and beeches hoar
Spread a huge vault of umbrage o'er,   10
Yet not so thick but yellow day
Makes through the leaves his splendid way,
And though in solemness of shade
The place is silent, but not sad;
Here as the Naiad of the spring   15

Tunes her deep-sounding liquid string,
And o'er the streamlet steals her song
Leading its sleepy waves along—
How rich to lay your limbs at ease
Under the humming trellises   20
Bowed down with clustering blooms and bees,
And leaning o'er some antique root
Murmur as old a ditty out,
To suit the low incessant roar,
The echo of some distant shore,   25
Where the sweet-bubbling waters run
To spread their foamy tippets on;
Or 'mid the dim green forest aisles
Still haughtier than cathedral piles,
Enwrapt in a fine horror stand   30
Musing upon the darkness grand,
Now looking sideways through the glooms
At ivied trunks shaped into tombs,
Now up the pillaring larches bare
Arching their Gothic boughs in air,   35
Perchance you wander on, in pain
To catch green glimpses of the plain,
Half glad to see the light again;
And wading through the seeded grass
Out to a sultry knoll you pass;   40
There with crossed arms in moral mood
Dreadless admire the cloistered wood
Returning your enhancèd frown,
Darker than night, stiller than stone.

But now the sun with dubious eye   45
Measures the downfall of the sky,
And pauses trembling on thy brow,
Olympus, ere he plunge below
Where ever-thundering Ocean lies
Spread out in blue immensities.   50

No stir the forest dames among,
No aspen wags a leafy tongue;
Absorbed in meditation stands
The cypress with her swathèd hands,
And even the restless Turin-tree   55
Seems lost in a like reverie;
Zephyr hath shut his scented mouth
And not a cloud moves from the South;
The hoary thistle keeps his beard
Chin-deep amid the sea-green sward,   60
And sleeps unbrushed by any wing
Save of that gaudy flickering thing
Too light to wake the blue-haired King;
Alone of the bright-coated crowd
This vanity is seen abroad,   65
Sunning his ashy pinions still
On flowery bank or ferny hill.
Now not a sole wood-note is heard,
The wild reed breathes no trumpet-word,
Even the home-happy cushat quells   70
Her note of comfort in the dells.
'Tis Noon!—and in the shadows warm
You only hear the gray-flies swarm,
You gaze between the earth and sky
With wide, unconscious, dizzy eye   75
And like the listless willow seem
Dropping yourself into a dream.

Dirge

Wail! wail ye o'er the dead!
　Wail! wail ye o'er her!
Youth's ta'en and Beauty's fled:
　O then deplore her!

Strew! strew ye, maidens, strew   5
　Sweet flowers and fairest,
Pale rose and pansy blue,
　Lily the rarest!

Lay, lay her gently down
　On her moss pillow,   10
While we our foreheads crown
　With the sad willow!

Raise, raise the song of woe,
　Youths, to her honour!
Fresh leaves and blossoms throw,   15
　Virgins, upon her!

Round, round the cypress bier,
　Where she lies sleeping,
On every turf a tear,
　Let us go weeping.   20

Wail! wail ye o'er the dead!
　Wail! wail ye o'er her!
Youth's ta'en and Beauty's fled:
　O then deplore her!

Final Chorus

Sweet Bards have told
That Mercy droppeth as the gentle rain
  From the benignant skies,
And that in simple-hearted times of old
  Praise unto Heaven again   5
Did in a fragrant cloud of incense rise.

Thus the great sun
Breathes his wide blessing over herb and flower,
  Which bloom as he doth burn,
And to his staid yet ever-moving throne   10
  They from the mead and bower
Offer a grateful perfume in return.

So then should we,
Whom Pity hath beheld with melting eye,
  Utter our hymns of praise   15
In solemn joy and meek triumphancy
  Unto the Powers on high;
Raise then the song of glory, shepherds, raise!

Siren Chorus

Troop home to silent grots and caves,
  Troop home! and mimic as you go
The mournful winding of the waves,
  Which to their dark abysses flow.

At this sweet hour all things beside 5
    In amorous pairs to covert creep,
The swans that brush the evening tide
    Homeward in snowy couples keep.

In his green den the murmuring seal
    Close by his sleek companion lies, 10
While singly we to bedward steal,
    And close in fruitless sleep our eyes.

In bowers of love men take their rest,
    In loveless bowers we sigh alone,
With bosom-friends are others blest, 15
    But we have none! but we have none!

To be or not to be

Annihilation, dark and everlasting!
Why this were well, I could exchange for this.
O how I long to throw this passion off!
And what so prompt, so near? The pilfering breeze,
That robs the scented valley of its sweets 5
And ravishes the poor defenceless flowers,
Winged by velleity can scarce o'ersweep
A few poor measures of the earth in th' hour
'Tis swift'st, while I by a little little step
And shrewd addition of the coffin-sheet 10
To keep me from the shivering touch of earth
Can pass from world to world! This is most well.

  To stand thus pinioned on the outside brink
Of the fool's horror, the dull cave of death,

That hides away the fleering heav'ns, the gaze   15
Of pitiless-hearted pitiers—to stand,
Loaden with weighty griefs and sallow cares,
Press'd by misfortunes innate and acquired,
And ere youth's rose hath summer'd on its stalk,
Turned to a wretched weed, wither'd and pale,   20
Stung by a venomous blast that bites my core,
Sickness, which binds me with an aching crown,
Encircling with its drowsy weight my head;
Last Poverty upon a carrion steed,
Cheering his black dogs Hunger and Nakedness   25
With slaughter-red mouths and sharp remorseless fangs
To tear my flesh, to strip my houseless form,
Lap my cold blood and hunt me to my grave—
To stand, I say, this world upon my back,
Galling my un-Atlantic shoulders, these fell dogs   30
Close at my heels pursuing—and the next
Small fluxion of the longitude of time,
My burthen hurl'd back to th' injurious skies,
My grim tormentors baffled in the teeth,
To rest in senseless quiet, joyless ease,   35
In the short compass that a corpse can measure
Laid stretch'd upon th' eternal bed of silence,
Pent up in futile boards or choked with clay—
I'll do't! I'll do't! Why what a fool was I
To whine and weep and play with tribulation,   40
When the cure lies in a phial or a pill!
Now, now, ye hideous band, ye coward crew,
That bend your horrors on a wretch like me,
Where's your dominion now, your terrors where?
Down with that sceptre, thou tyrannic fool,   45
That sways it o'er my health! Stand back, stand back,
Yellow-eyed Melancholy and black Despair,
The gulf is at your foot! And thou, thin Poverty,
Charm off thy dogs, and pull thy courser's neck

Down to his knee! Insatiate! What, wilt follow me   50
From yon dread cliff that breaks the midway air
Into yon gorge? Perdition gapes beneath
And stretches wider its immoderate jaws
For thee and these. Have I appall'd thee, fiend?
Dar'st thou not follow me? 'Tis well! Begone!   55
There is your cease. There my redemption lies.
I'll leap, though sooty hell should grin beneath
Or thunder roll above, to shake the Mercy-seat!

A Sea Dream

I seem like one lost in a deep blue sea
Down, down beneath the billows many a mile,
Where nought of their loud eloquence is heard,
Save a dead murmur of the rushing waves
Fleeting above, more silent than no sound.   5
Over my head, as high as to the moon,
The tall insuperable waters rise
Pure and translucent, through whose total depth
The imminent stars shoot unrefracted rays
And whiten all the bottom of the flood.   10
The sea-bed hath a scenery of its own
And nought less wondrous than the realms of air,
Hills, dells, rocks, groves, sea-flowers and sedgy caves
In crystal armour lock'd, scatter'd around!
Here like a mortal tenant of the sea,   15
Or fabulous merman, hermit of the wave,
I stand, the sad surveyor of the scene,
Alone, amid the deserts of the deep.

To my Tyrant

Thou, at whose feet I waste my soul in sighs,
Before whose beauty my proud heart is meek,
Thou, who makest dovelike my fierce falcon-eyes,
And palest the rose of my Lancastrian cheek
With one cold smile about thy budded mouth,   5
O that my harmless vengeance I could wreak
On that pale rival bloom of thine! The South
Raves not more fell, prisoned an April week,
To feed on lily-banks, than I to prey
Some greedy minutes on that blossom white,   10
Whose gentle ravage thou'dst too long delay!
O when these roses of our cheeks unite,
Will't not a summer-happy season be
If not for England, in sweet sooth for me!

It is not Beauty I demand

It is not Beauty I demand,
   A crystal brow, the moon's despair,
Nor the snow's daughter, a white hand,
   Nor mermaid's yellow pride of hair.

Tell me not of your starry eyes,   5
   Your lips that seem on roses fed,
Your breasts where Cupid trembling lies,
   Nor sleeps for kissing of his bed.

A bloomy pair of vermeil cheeks,
  Like Hebe's in her ruddiest hours,   10
A breath that softer music speaks
  Than summer winds a-wooing flowers.

These are but gauds; nay, what are lips?
  Coral beneath the ocean-stream,
Whose brink when your adventurer sips   15
  Full oft he perisheth on them.

And what are cheeks but ensigns oft
  That wave hot youth to fields of blood?
Did Helen's breast though ne'er so soft
  Do Greece or Ilium any good?   20

Eyes can with baleful ardour burn,
  Poison can breath that erst perfumed,
There's many a white hand holds an urn
  With lovers' hearts to dust consumed.

For crystal brows—there's naught within,   25
  They are but empty cells for pride;
He who the Siren's hair would win
  Is mostly strangled in the tide.

Give me, instead of beauty's bust,
  A tender heart, a loyal mind,   30
Which with temptation I could trust,
  Yet never linked with error find.

One in whose gentle bosom I
  Could pour my secret heart of woes,
Like the care-burthened honey-fly   35
  That hides his murmurs in the rose.

'Twas not thy smile that brib'd my partial reason,
Tho' never maiden's smile was good as thine:—
Nor did I to thy goodness wed my heart,
Dreaming of soft delights and honied kisses,   10
Although thou wert complete in every part,
A stainless paradise of holy blisses:
I lov'd thee for the lovely soul thou art,—
Thou canst not change so true a love as this is.

Long time a child . . .

Long time a child, and still a child, when years
Had painted manhood on my cheek, was I;
For yet I lived like one not born to die;
A thriftless prodigal of smiles and tears,
No hope I needed, and I knew no fears.   5
But sleep, though sweet, is only sleep, and waking,
I waked to sleep no more, at once o'ertaking
The vanguard of my age, with all arrears
Of duty on my back. Nor child, nor man,
Nor youth, nor sage, I find my head is grey,   10
For I have lost the race I never ran:
A rathe December blights my lagging May;
And still I am a child, tho' I be old,
Time is my debtor for my years untold.

Youth, love, and mirth, what are they . . .

Youth, love, and mirth, what are they—but the portion,
Wherewith the Prodigal left his Father's home,
Through foreign lands in search of bliss to roam,
And find each seeming joy a mere abortion,
And every smile, an agonised distortion   5
Of pale Repentance' face, and barren womb?
Youth, love, and mirth! too quickly they consume
Their passive substance, and their small proportion
Of fleeting life, in memory's backward view,
Still dwindles to a point, a twinkling star,   10
Long gleaming o'er the onward course of Being;
That tells us whence we came, and where we are,
And tells us too, how swiftly we are fleeing
From all we were and loved, when life was new.

November

The mellow year is hasting to its close;
The little birds have almost sung their last,
Their small notes twitter in the dreary blast—
That shrill-piped harbinger of early snows;
The patient beauty of the scentless rose,   5
Oft with the Morn's hoar crystal quaintly glass'd,
Hangs, a pale mourner for the summer past,
And makes a little summer where it grows:
In the chill sunbeam of the faint brief day
The dusky waters shudder as they shine,   10
The russet leaves obstruct the straggling way
Of oozy brooks, which no deep banks define,
And the gaunt woods, in ragged, scant array,
Wrap their old limbs with sombre ivy twine.

Night

The crackling embers on the hearth are dead;
The indoor note of industry is still;
The latch is fast; upon the window sill
The small birds wait not for their daily bread;
The voiceless flowers—how quietly they shed   5
Their nightly odours;—and the household rill
Murmurs continuous dulcet sounds that fill
The vacant expectation, and the dread
Of listening night. And haply now she sleeps;
For all the garrulous noises of the air   10
Are hushed in peace; the soft dew silent weeps,
Like hopeless lovers for a maid so fair—
Oh! that I were the happy dream that creeps
To her soft heart, to find my image there.

I thank my God . . .

I thank my God because my hairs are grey!
But have grey hairs brought wisdom? Doth the flight
Of summer birds, departed while the light
Of life is lingering on the middle way,
Predict the harvest nearer by a day?   5
Will the rank weeds of hopeless appetite
Droop at the glance and venom of the blight
That made the vermeil bloom, the flush so gay,
Dim and unlovely as a dead worm's shroud?
Or is my heart, that, wanting hope, has lost   10
The strength and rudder of resolve, at peace?
Is it no longer wrathful, vain and proud?
Is it a Sabbath, or untimely frost,
That makes the labour of the soul to cease?

'Tis strange to me . . .

'Tis strange to me, who long have seen no face,
That was not like a book, whose every page
I knew by heart, a kindly common-place—
And faithful record of progressive age—
To wander forth, and view an unknown race;   5
Of all that I have been, to find no trace,
No footstep of my by-gone pilgrimage.
Thousands I pass, and no one stays his pace
To tell me that the day is fair, or rainy—
Each one his object seeks with anxious chase,   10
And I have not a common hope with any—
Thus like one drop of oil upon a flood,
In uncommunicating solitude—
Single am I amid the countless many.

If I have sinn'd in act . . .

If I have sinn'd in act, I may repent;
If I have err'd in thought, I may disclaim
My silent error, and yet feel no shame—
But if my soul, big with an ill intent,
Guilty in will, by fate be innocent,   5
Or being bad, yet murmurs at the curse
And incapacity of being worse
That makes my hungry passion still keep Lent
In keen expectance of a Carnival;
Where, in all worlds, that round the sun revolve   10
And shed their influence on this passive ball,
Abides a power that can my soul absolve?
Could any sin survive, and be forgiven—
One sinful wish would make a hell of heaven.

What is young passion . . .

What is young Passion but a gusty breeze
Ruffling the surface of a shallow flood?
A vernal motion of the vital blood,
That sweetly gushes from a heart at ease,
As sugar'd sap in spicy-budding trees?   5
And tho' a wish be born with every morrow,
And fondest dreams full oft are types of sorrow,
Eyes that can smile may weep just when they please.
But adult Passion, centred far within,
Hid from the moment's venom and its balm,   10
Works with the fell inherency of sin,

Nor feels the joy of morn, nor evening calm:
For morn nor eve can change that fiery gloom
That glares within the spirit's living tomb.

Time was when I could weep . . .

Time was when I could weep; but now all care
Is gone—yet have I gazed 'till sense deceived
Almost assures me that her bosom heav'd;
And o'er those features—as the lightest air
On summer sea—Life play'd, did they but bear   5
One trace of Mind, faintly in sleep perceiv'd,
Wand'ring, from earthly impulse unreliev'd—
Through regions of Emotion, wild or fair.
Her mind is gone! and now, while over all
A ghastly dreaming quiet seems to lie,   10
All Sounds subdued to mournful harmony,
My heart is tranquil; sunk beyond the Call
Of Hope or Fear; and still must deeper fall,
Down—down with Time, till e'en remembrance die.

I fear you think . . .

I fear you think (when friends by fate are parted
Fraught evermore in fear) that I forget
The small snug parlour where so oft we met
And that wee garden gate whence I have started
Oft on my homeward pad—not quite deserted   5
Though wending lonely through the dark and wet.
Thy voice was in mine ear, thy hand was yet
Thrilling in mine and made me lion hearted.
Nor can the blessing ever pass to nought
Which thou, dear Bessy, gavest so kind and free,   10
When far beyond the wide Atlantic Sea
Thy soul with recent care and knowledge fraught
Had for the old world many a loving thought
And yet could spare a loving thought for me.—

Full well I know . . .

Full well I know—my Friends—ye look on me
A living spectre of my Father dead—
Had I not borne his name, had I not fed
On him, as one leaf trembling on a tree,
A woeful waste had been my minstrelsy—   5
Yet have I sung of maidens newly wed
And I have wished that hearts too sharply bled
Should throb with less of pain, and heave more free
By my endeavour. Still alone I sit
Counting each thought as Miser counts a penny,   10
Wishing to spend my penny-worth of wit
On antic wheel of fortune like a Zany:
You love me for my sire, to you unknown,
Revere me for his sake, and love me for my own.

How shall a man fore-doomed . . .

How shall a man fore-doomed to lone estate,
Untimely old, irreverently grey,
Much like a patch of dusty snow in May,
Dead sleeping in a hollow, all too late—
How shall so poor a thing congratulate   5
The blest completion of a patient wooing,
Or how commend a younger man for doing
What ne'er to do hath been his fault or fate?
There is a fable, that I once did read,
Of a bad angel, that was someway good,   10
And therefore on the brink of Heaven he stood,
Looking each way, and no way could proceed;
Till at the last he purged away his sin
By loving all the joy he saw within.

Regeneration

I need a cleansing change within—
My life must once again begin—
New hope I need, and youth renew'd,
And more than human fortitude,—
New faith, new love, and strength to cast   5
Away the fetters of the past.

Ah! why did fabling Poets tell
That Lethe only flows in Hell?
As if, in truth, there was no river,
Whereby the leper may be clean,   10

But that which flows and flows for ever,
And crawls along, unheard, unseen,
Whence brutish spirits, in contagious shoals,
Quaff the dull drench of apathetic souls.

Ah, no! but Lethe flows aloft   15
With lulling murmur, kind and soft
As voice which sinners send to heaven
When first they feel their sins forgiven:
Its every drop as bright and clear
As if indeed it were a tear,   20
Shed by the lovely Magdalen
For Him that was despised of men.

It is the only fount of bliss
In all the human wilderness—
It is the true Bethesda—solely   25
Endued with healing might, and holy:—
Not once a year, but evermore—
Not one, but all men to restore.

Song

The earliest wish I ever knew
Was woman's kind regard to win;
I felt it long ere passion grew,
Ere such a wish could be a sin.

And still it lasts;—the yearning ache   5
No cure has found, no comfort known:
If she did love, 'twas for my sake,
She could not love me for her own.

25

To Somebody

'And the imperial votaress passed on
In maiden meditation fancy free.'
Shakespeare

I blame not her, because my soul
   Is not like her's,—a treasure
Of self-sufficing good,—a whole
   Complete in every measure.

I charge her not with cruel pride,   5
   With self-admired disdain;
Too happy she, or to deride,
   Or to perceive my pain.

I blame her not—she cannot know
   What she did never prove: 10
Her streams of sweetness purely flow
   Unblended yet with love.

No fault hath she, that I desire
   What she cannot conceive;
For she is made of bliss entire,   15
   And I was born to grieve.

And though she hath a thousand wiles,
   And, in a moment's space,
As fast as light, a thousand smiles
   Come showering from her face,—   20

Those winsome smiles, those sunny looks,
   Her heart securely deems,
Cold as the flashing of the brooks
   In the cold moonlight beams.

Her sweet affections, free as wind,   25
    Nor fear, nor craving feel;
No secret hollow hath her mind
    For passion to reveal.

Her being's law is gentle bliss,
    Her purpose, and her duty;   30
And quiet joy her loveliness,
    And gay delight her beauty.

Then let her walk in mirthful pride,
    Dispensing joy and sadness,
By her light spirit fortified   35
    In panoply of gladness.

The joy she gives shall still be her's,
    The sorrow shall be mine;
Such debt the earthly heart incurs
    That pants for the divine.   40

But better 'tis to love, I ween,
    And die of slow despair,
Than die, and never to have seen
    A maid so lovely fair.

To ——

I love thee—none may know how well,
And yet—I would not have thee love me;
To thy good heart 'twere very hell,
To love me dear, and not approve me.

Whate'er thou lov'st it is not *thine*,   5
But 'tis *thyself*—then sad it were, love,
If thou for every sin of mine,
Should weep, repent,—mayhap, despair—love.

Then love me not—thou can'st not scorn;
And mind—I do not bid thee hate me;   10
And if I die, oh, do not mourn,
But if I live, *do* new *create* me.

Expertus Loquitur

"'Tis sad experience speaks'

There never was a blessing, or a curse,
So sweet, so cruel, as a knack of verse.
When the smug stripling finds the way to rhyme,
Glad as the wild bee 'mid a bed of thyme;
With dulcet murmuring, all a summer's day,   5
With many a scrap of many a purposed lay—
Fitful, yet gentle, as a summer wind,
Pleased with himself, and pleased with all mankind,
Sure of the praise which partial friends bestow,
He breathes in bliss, if bliss may be below.   10

Pass some few years—and see where all will end.
The hireling scribe, estranged from every friend,
Or if one friend remain, 'tis one so brave,
He will not quit the wreck he cannot save;
The good man's pity, and the proud man's scorn,   15
The Muse's vagabond, he roams forlorn—
Thought, wit, invention, tenderness have left him,
All wealth of mind, save empty rhyme, bereft him—

Yet write he must, for still he needs must eat—
Retail fantastic sorrow by the sheet—   20
Sing in his garret of the flowery grove,
And pinch'd with hunger, wail the woes of love—
Oh may all Christian souls while yet 'tis time,
Renounce the World, the Flesh, the Devil, and Rhyme.

By a Friend

I have heard thy sweet voice in the song,
    And listen'd with delight—
I've seen thee in the glittering throng,
    The fairest 'midst the bright—
I've mark'd thee smile on gallants gay,   5
    And envied them the lot,
While from the crowd I turn'd away,
    Alone regarded not.

Oh, Lady! it were vain, I own,
    To hope for charms like thine!   10
The brow that would beseem a crown
    Will frown on love like mine:
That form of light—that heavenly face,
    Those eyes of sweetest hue,
Were form'd some kingly throne to grace,   15
    And not for me to sue.

Yet, though forbidden by despair
    The dream of happier hours—
As once I wreath'd thy sunny hair   20
    With Summer's brightest flowers—

I'll follow still, with love unseen,
   Thy smile, thy voice's tone;
My heart shall own no other queen,
   But worship thee alone.

Poietes Apoietes

No hope have I to live a deathless name,
   A power immortal in the world of mind,
A sun to light with intellectual flame
   The universal soul of human kind.

Not mine the skill in memorable phrase,   5
   The hidden truths of passion to reveal,
To bring to light the intermingling ways,
   By which unconscious motives darkling steal;

To show how forms the sentient heart affect,
   How thoughts and feelings mutually combine,   10
How oft the pure, impassive intellect
   Shares the mischances of his mortal shrine.

Nor can I summon from the dark abyss
   Of time, the spirit of forgotten things,
Bestow unfading life on transient bliss—   15
   Bid memory live with 'healing on its wings'.

Or give a substance to the haunting shades,
   Whose visitation shames the vulgar earth,
Before whose light the ray of morning fades,
   And hollow yearning chills the soul of mirth.   20

I have no charm to renovate the youth
   Of old authentic dictates of the heart,—
To wash the wrinkles from the face of Truth,
   And out of Nature form creative Art.

Divinest Poesy!—'tis thine to make   25
   Age young—youth old—to baffle tyrant Time,
From antique strains the hoary dust to shake,
   And with familiar grace to crown new rhyme.

Long have I loved thee—long have loved in vain,
   Yet large the debt my spirit owes to thee,   30
Thou wreath'dst my first hours in a rosy chain,
   Rocking the cradle of my infancy.

The lovely images of earth and sky
   From thee I learn'd within my soul to treasure;
And the strong magic of thy minstrelsy   35
   Charms the world's tempest to a sweet, sad measure.

Nor Fortune's spite   nor hopes that once have been—
   Hopes which no power of Fate can give again,—
Not the sad sentence—that my life must wean
   From dear domestic joys—nor all the train   40

Of pregnant ills—and penitential harms
   That dog the rear of youth unwisely wasted,
Can dim the lustre of thy stainless charms,
   Or sour the sweetness that in thee I tasted.

Death-bed Reflections of Michelangelo

Not that my hand could make of stubborn stone
Whate'er of Gods the shaping thought conceives;
Not that my skill by pictured lines hath shown
All terrors that the guilty soul believes;
Not that my art, by blended light and shade,   5
Express'd the world as it was newly made;
Not that my verse profoundest truth could teach,
In the soft accents of the lover's speech;
Not that I rear'd a temple for mankind,
To meet and pray in, borne by every wind—   10
Affords me peace—I count my gain but loss,
For that vast love, that hangs upon the Cross.

There was a cot . . .

There was a cot, a little rustic home,
Which oft I used to pass in careless youth,
Where a sweet child was growing like a flower
In the high fissure of a mossy crag,
Giving a kind and human loveliness   5
To bleakest solitude—I know not why
In all my rambles, still my steps were led
To that lone dwelling,—still—if e'er I missed
The little maiden with her sun-burn'd face,
Her rosy face that glowed with summer brown,   10
Quick glancing through the lattice, my heart sank
And all that day my thoughts were matterless
As if defrauded of their daily bread;
But when she lilted from the lowly door

Tossing her burden of crisp, curly locks   15
That kept her arms in pretty motion still
To give free prospect to her wild blue eyes,
My soul was glad within me, as the deep
Glows with the young light of the sudden Sun,
For three long years I watch'd her, and she seem'd   20
To greet my coming as a natural thing,
The punctual quitrent of unfailing time.

I dreamed that buried in my fellow clay

I dreamed that buried in my fellow clay
Close by a common beggar's side I lay,
And as so mean an object shock'd my pride,
Thus like a corpse of consequence I cry'd,
'Scoundrel, begone, and henceforth touch me not,   5
More manners learn and at a distance rot.'
'How! scoundrel!' with a hautier tone cry'd he,
'Proud lump of earth, I scorn thy words and thee,
Here all are equal, now thy case is mine,
This is my rotting place, and that is thine.'   10

To love—and not be loved . . .

To love—and not be loved—is such my Fate?
Did God!—Oh! Could that gracious Sire create
A soul to feel and love his excellence
Yes—to adorn him with a faith intense
To love him in the earth and sky and sea,   5
Yet doom that soul to perish utterly?

With much of fear . . .

With much of fear, yet not without
Enough of hope to strive with doubt
I close December's eighteenth day.
What must I do? Fear—hope—and pray.
                    (18 December 1841)

Ah! woeful impotence of weak resolve

Ah! woeful impotence of weak resolve,
Recorded rashly to the writer's shame,
Days pass away, and Time's large orbs revolve,
And every day beholds me still the same,
Till oft neglected purpose loses aim,   5
And hope becomes a flat unheeded lie,
And conscience weary with the work of blame,
In seeming slumber droops her wistful eye
As if she would resign her unregarded ministry.

Presentiment

Something has my heart to say
Something on my breast does weigh
That when I would full fain be gay
        Still pulls me back.

Something evil does this load   5
Most assuredly forebode,
So my experience sadly shew'd
    Too well I know.

Sometime, as if with mocking guile
The pain departs a little while,   10
Then I can dance and sing and smile
    With merry glee—

But soon, too soon it comes again
The sulky, stifling, leaden pain,
As a black cloud is big with rain   15
    'Tis big with woe.

All I ask is but to know
The depth and nature of the woe.
I hope not for a wind to blow
    The cloud away.   20

I hear an inarticulate sound
Wherein no fixed sense is found
But sorrow, sorrow without bound
    Of what or where.

I have been cherish'd . . .

I have been cherish'd, and forgiven
    By many tender-hearted,
'Twas for the sake of one in Heaven
    Of *him* that is departed.

Because I bear my Father's name   5
    I am not quite despised,
My little legacy of fame
    I've not yet realized.

And yet if you should praise myself
    I'll tell you, I had rather   10
You'd give your love to me, poor elf,
    Your praise to my great father.

When we are dead . . .

When we are dead and gone to Davy's Locker,
Still shall thy name survive, great Goose of Cocker.

Epitaph on an honest hostess

Stranger, who e'er thou art, respect this stone.
The name it bears may be to thee unknown
And to the world. But it to *one* was dear
Or else it never had been sculptured here.
It will not ask thee for her soul to pray;   5
Pray for thy self, and all, and go thy way.

On a dissolution of Ministry

Shout Britain, raise a joyful shout,
The Tyrant Tories all are out—
Deluded Britons—cease your din—
For lo—the scoundrel Whigs are in.

He lived amidst th'untrodden ways

He lived amidst th'untrodden ways
　　To Rydal Lake that lead:—
A bard whom there were none to praise
　　And very few to read.

Behind a cloud his mystic sense,　　　　　　　5
　　Deep-hidden, who can spy?
Bright as the night, when not a star
　　Is shining in the sky.

Unread his works—his 'Milk-white Doe'
　　With dust is dark and dim;　　　　　　　10
It's still in Longman's shop, and Oh
　　The Difference to him!

THOMAS HOOD

I Remember, I Remember

I remember, I remember,
The house where I was born,
The little window where the sun
Came peeping in at morn;
He never came a wink too soon,   5
Nor brought too long a day,
But now, I often wish the night
Had borne my breath away!

I remember, I remember,
The roses, red and white,   10
The vi'lets, and the lily-cups,
Those flowers made of light!
The lilacs where the robin built,
And where my brother set
The laburnum on his birthday,—   15
The tree is living yet!

I remember, I remember,
Where I was used to swing,
And thought the air must rush as fresh
To swallows on the wing;   20
My spirit flew in feathers then,
That is so heavy now,
And summer pools could hardly cool
The fever on my brow!

I remember, I remember,   25
The fir trees dark and high;
I used to think their slender tops
Were close against the sky:
It was a childish ignorance,
But now 'tis little joy   30
To know I'm farther off from heav'n
Than when I was a boy.

Ode: Autumn

I saw old Autumn in the misty morn
Stand shadowless like Silence, listening
To silence, for no lonely bird would sing
Into his hollow ear from woods forlorn,
Nor lowly hedge nor solitary thorn;—   5
Shaking his languid locks all dewy bright
With tangled gossamer that fell by night,
    Pearling his coronet of golden corn.

Where are the songs of Summer?—With the sun,
Oping the dusky eyelids of the south,   10
Till shade and silence waken up as one,
And Morning sings with a warm odorous mouth,
Where are the merry birds?—Away, away,
On panting wings through the inclement skies,
    Lest owls should prey   15
    Undazzled at noon-day.
And tear with horny beak their lustrous eyes.

Where are the blooms of Summer?—In the west,
Blushing their last to the last sunny hours,

When the mild Eve by sudden Night is prest   20
Like tearful Proserpine, snatch'd from her flow'rs
    To a most gloomy breast.

Where is the pride of Summer,—the green pine,—
The many, many leaves all twinkling?—Three
    On the moss'd elm; three on the naked lime   25
Trembling,—and one upon the old oak tree!
    Where is the Dryads' immortality?—
Gone into mournful cypress and dark yew,
Or wearing the long gloomy Winter through
    In the smooth holly's green eternity.   30
The squirrel gloats on his accomplish'd hoard,
The ants have brimm'd their garners with ripe grain,
    And honey bees have stor'd
The sweets of Summer in their luscious cells;
The swallows all have wing'd across the main;   35
But here the Autumn melancholy dwells,
    And sighs her tearful spells
Amongst the sunless shadows of the plain.
    Alone, alone,
      Upon a mossy stone,   40
She sits and reckons up the dead and gone
With the last leaves for a love-rosary,
Whilst all the wither'd world looks drearily,
Like a dim picture of the drowned past
In the hush'd mind's mysterious far away,   45
Doubtful what ghostly thing will steal the last
Into that distance, grey upon the grey.
O go and sit with her, and be o'ershaded
Under the languid downfall of her hair:
She wears a coronal of flowers faded   50
Upon her forehead, and a face of care;—
There is enough of wither'd every where
To make her bower,—and enough of gloom;

There is enough of sadness to invite,
If only for the rose that died,—whose doom 55
Is Beauty's,—she that with the living bloom
Of conscious cheeks most beautifies the light;—
There is enough of sorrowing, and quite
Enough of bitter fruits the earth doth bear,—
Enough of chilly droppings for her bowl; 60
Enough of fear and shadowy despair,
To frame her cloudy prison for the soul!

The Last Man

'Twas in the year two thousand and one,
A pleasant morning of May,
I sat on the gallows-tree all alone,
A chaunting a merry lay,—
To think how the pest had spared my life, 5
To sing with the larks that day!

When up the heath came a jolly knave,
Like a scarecrow, all in rags:
It made me crow to see his old duds
All abroad in the wind, like flags:— 10
So up he came to the timbers' foot
And pitch'd down his greasy bags.—

Good Lord! how blythe the old beggar was!
At pulling out his scraps,—
The very sight of his broken orts 15
Made a work in his wrinkled chaps:
'Come down,' says he, 'you Newgate bird,
And have a taste of my snaps!'——

Then down the rope, like a tar from the mast,
I slided, and by him stood; 20
But I wished myself on the gallows again
When I smelt that beggar's food,
A foul beef-bone and a mouldy crust;
'Oh!' quoth he, 'the heavens are good!'

Then after this grace he cast him down: 25
Says I, 'You'll get sweeter air
A pace or two off, on the windward side,'
For the felons' bones lay there.
But he only laugh'd at the empty skulls,
And offered them part of his fare. 30

'I never harm'd *them*, and they won't harm me:
Let the proud and the rich be cravens!'
I did not like that strange beggar man,
He look'd so up at the heavens.
Anon he shook out his empty old poke; 35
'There's the crumbs,' saith he, 'for the ravens!'

It made me angry to see his face,
It had such a jesting look;
But while I made up my mind to speak,
A small case-bottle he took: 40
Quoth he, 'though I gather the green water-cress,
My drink is not of the brook!'

Full manners-like he tender'd the dram;
Oh, it came of a dainty cask!
But, whenever it came to his turn to pull, 45
'Your leave, good sir, I must ask;
But I always wipe the brim with my sleeve,
When a hangman sups at my flask!'

And then he laugh'd so loudly and long,
The churl was quite out of breath;   50
I thought the very Old One was come
To mock me before my death,
And wish'd I had buried the dead men's bones
That were lying about the heath!

But the beggar gave me a jolly clap—   55
'Come, let us pledge each other,
For all the wide world is dead beside,
And we are brother and brother—
I've a yearning for thee in my heart,
As if we had come of one mother.   60

'I've a yearning for thee in my heart
That almost makes me weep,
For as I pass'd from town to town
The folks were all stone-asleep,—
But when I saw thee sitting aloft,   65
It made me both laugh and leap!'

Now a curse (I thought) be on his love,
And a curse upon his mirth,—
An' if it were not for that beggar man
I'd be the King of the earth,—   70
But I promis'd myself an hour should come
To make him rue his birth—

So down we sat and bous'd again
Till the sun was in mid-sky,
When, just when the gentle west-wind came,   75
We hearken'd a dismal cry;
'Up, up, on the tree,' quoth the beggar man,
'Till these horrible dogs go by!'

And, lo! from the forest's far-off skirts,
They came all yelling for gore,   80
A hundred hounds pursuing at once,
And a panting hart before,
Till he sunk down at the gallows' foot,
And there his haunches they tore!

His haunches they tore, without a horn   85
To tell when the chase was done;
And there was not a single scarlet coat
To flaunt it in the sun!—
I turn'd, and look'd at the beggar man,
And his tears dropt one by one!   90

And with curses sore he chid at the hounds,
Till the last dropt out of sight,
Anon, saith he, 'Let's down again,
And ramble for our delight,
For the world's all free, and we may choose   95
A right oozie barn for to-night!'

With that, he set up his staff on end,
And it fell with the point due West;
So we far'd that way to a city great,
Where the folks had died of the pest—   100
It was fine to enter in house and hall
Wherever it liked me best;

For the porters all were stiff and cold,
And could not lift their heads;
And when we came where their masters lay,   105
The rats leapt out of the beds;
The grandest palaces in the land
Were as free as workhouse sheds.

But the beggar man made a mumping face,
And knocked at every gate: 110
It made me curse to hear how he whined,
So our fellowship turned to hate,
And I bade him walk the world by himself,
For I scorn'd so humble a mate!

So *he* turn'd right, and *I* turn'd left,   115
As if we had never met;
And I chose a fair stone house for myself,
For the city was all to let;
And for three brave holidays drank my fill
Of the choicest that I could get.   120

And because my jerkin was coarse and worn,
I got me a properer vest;
It was purple velvet, stitch'd o'er with gold,
And a shining star at the breast!—
'Twas enough to fetch old Joan from her grave   125
To see me so purely drest!

But Joan was dead and under the mould,
And every buxom lass;
In vain I watch'd, at the window pane
For a Christian soul to pass!   130
But sheep and kine wander'd up the street,
And browz'd on the new-come grass.—

When lo! I spied the old beggar man,
And lustily he did sing!—
His rags were lapp'd in a scarlet cloak,   135
And a crown he had like a King;
So he stept right up before my gate
And danc'd me a saucy fling!

Heaven mend us all!—but, within my mind,
I had killed him then and there;   140
To see him lording so braggart-like
That was born to his beggar's fare,
And how he had stolen the royal crown
His betters were meant to wear.

But God forbid that a thief should die   145
Without his share of the laws!
So I nimbly whipt my tackle out,
And soon tied up his claws,—
I was judge myself, and jury, and all,
And solemnly tried the cause.   150

But the beggar man would not plead, but cried
Like a babe without its corals,
For he knew how hard it is apt to go
When the law and a thief have quarrels,—
There was not a Christian soul alive   155
To speak a word for his morals.

Oh, how gaily I doff'd my costly gear,
And put on my work-day clothes;
I was tired of such a long Sunday life,—
And never was one of the sloths;   160
But the beggar man grumbled a weary deal,
And made many crooked mouths.

So I haul'd him off to the gallows' foot,
And blinded him in his bags;
'Twas a weary job to heave him up,   165
For a doom'd man always lags;
But by ten of the clock he was off his legs
In the wind, and airing his rags!

So there he hung, and there I stood,
The LAST MAN left alive,   170
To have my own will of all the earth:
Quoth I, now I shall thrive!
But when was ever honey made
With one bee in a hive?

My conscience began to gnaw my heart   175
Before the day was done,
For other men's lives had all gone out,
Like candles in the sun!—
But it seem'd as if I had broke, at last,
A thousand necks in one!   180

So I went and cut his body down
To bury it decentlie;—
God send there were any good soul alive
To do the like by me!
But the wild dogs came with terrible speed,   185
And bayed me up the tree!

My sight was like a drunkard's sight,
And my head began to swim,
To see their jaws all white with foam,
Like the ravenous ocean brim;—   190
But when the wild dogs trotted away
Their jaws were bloody and grim!

Their jaws were bloody and grim, good Lord!
But the beggar man, where was he?—
There was naught of him but some ribbons of rags   195
Below the gallows' tree!—
I know the Devil, when I am dead,
Will send his hounds for me!—

47

I've buried my babies one by one,
And dug the deep hole for Joan,   200
And covered the faces of kith and kin,
And felt the old churchyard stone
Go cold to my heart, full many a time,
But I never felt so lone!

For the lion and Adam were company,   205
And the tiger him beguiled:
But the simple kine are foes to my life,
And the household brutes are wild.
If the veriest cur would lick my hand,
I could love it like a child!   210

And the beggar man's ghost besets my dream,
At night to make me madder,—
And my wretched conscience within my breast,
Is like a stinging adder;—
I sigh when I pass the gallows' foot,   215
And look at the rope and ladder!—

For hanging looks sweet,—but, alas! in vain
My desperate fancy begs,—
I must turn my cup of sorrows quite up,
And drink it to the dregs,—   220
For there is not another man alive,
In the world, to pull my legs!

from *The Plea of the Midsummer Fairies*

I

'Twas in that mellow season of the year,
When the hot Sun singes the yellow leaves
Till they be gold,—and with a broader sphere
The Moon looks down on Ceres and her sheaves;
When more abundantly the spider weaves,   5
And the cold wind breathes from a chillier clime;
That forth I fared, on one of those still eves,
Touch'd with the dewy sadness of the time,
To think how the bright months had spent their prime.

II

So that, wherever I address'd my way,   10
I seem'd to track the melancholy feet
Of him that is the Father of Decay,
And spoils at once the sour weed and the sweet;—
Wherefore regretfully I made retreat
To some unwasted regions of my brain,   15
Charm'd with the light of summer and the heat,
And bade that bounteous season bloom again,
And sprout fresh flowers in mine own domain.

III

It was a shady and sequester'd scene,
Like those famed gardens of Boccaccio,   20
Planted with his own laurels evergreen,
And roses that for endless summer blow;
And there were founting springs to overflow

Their marble basins,—and cool green arcades
Of tall o'erarching sycamores, to throw   25
Athwart the dappled path their dancing shades,—
With timid coneys cropping the green blades.

IV

And there were crystal pools, peopled with fish,
Argent and gold; and some of Tyrian skin,
Some crimson-barr'd;—and ever at a wish   30
They rose obsequious till the wave grew thin
As glass upon their backs, and then dived in,
Quenching their ardent scales in watery gloom;
Whilst others with fresh hues row'd forth to win
My changeable regard,—for so we doom   35
Things born of thought to vanish or to bloom.

V

And there were many birds of many dyes,
From tree to tree still faring to and fro,
And stately peacocks with their splendid eyes,
And gorgeous pheasants with their golden glow,   40
Like Iris just bedabbled in her bow,
Besides some vocalists, without a name,
That oft on fairy errands come and go,
With accents magical;—and all were tame,
And peckled at my hand where'er I came.   45

VI

And for my sylvan company, in lieu
Of Pampinea with her lively peers,
Sat Queen Titania with her pretty crew,
All in their liveries quaint, with elfin gears,

For she was gracious to my childish years,   50
And made me free of her enchanted round;
Wherefore this dreamy scene she still endears,
And plants her court upon a verdant mound,
Fenced with umbrageous woods and groves profound.

The Two Peacocks of Bedfont

I

Alas! that breathing Vanity should go
    Where Pride is buried,—like its very ghost,
Uprisen from the naked bones below,
    In novel flesh, clad in the silent boast
Of gaudy silk that flutters to and fro,   5
    Shedding its chilling superstition most
On young and ignorant natures—as it wont
To haunt the peaceful churchyard of Bedfont!

II

Each Sabbath morning, at the hour of prayer,
    Behold two maidens, up the quiet green   10
Shining, far distant, in the summer air
    That flaunts their dewy robes and breathes between
Their downy plumes,—sailing as if they were
    Two far-off ships,—until they brush between
The churchyard's humble walls, and watch and wait   15
On either side of the wide open'd gate.

III

And there they stand—with haughty necks before
　God's holy house, that points towards the skies—
Frowning reluctant duty from the poor,
　And tempting homage from unthoughtful eyes: 20
And Youth looks lingering from the temple door,
　Breathing its wishes in unfruitful sighs,
With pouting lips,—forgetful of the grace,
Of health, and smiles, on the heart-conscious face;—

IV

Because that Wealth, which has no bliss beside,   25
　May wear the happiness of rich attire;
And those two sisters, in their silly pride,
　May change the soul's warm glances for the fire
Of lifeless diamonds;—and for health deny'd,—
　With art, that blushes at itself, inspire   30
Their languid cheeks—and flourish in a glory
That has no life in life, nor after-story.

V

The aged priest goes shaking his grey hair
　In meekest censuring, and turns his eye
Earthward in grief, and heavenward in pray'r,   35
　And sighs, and clasps his hands, and passes by.
Good-hearted man! what sullen soul would wear
　Thy sorrow for a garb, and constantly
Put on thy censure, that might win the praise
Of one so grey in goodness and in days?   40

Also the solemn clerk partakes the shame
   Of this ungodly shine of human pride,
And sadly blends his reverence and blame
   In one grave bow, and passes with a stride
Impatient:—many a red-hooded dame   45
   Turns her pain'd head, but her glance, aside
From wanton dress, and marvels o'er again,
That heaven hath no wet judgments for the vain.

VII

'I have a lily in the bloom at home,'
   Quoth one, 'and by the blessed Sabbath day   50
I'll pluck my lily in its pride, and come
   And read a lesson upon vain array;—
And when stiff silks are rustling up, and some
   Give place, I'll shake it in proud eyes and say
Making my reverence,—"Ladies, an' you please,   55
King Solomon's not half so fine as these." '

Then her meek partner, who has nearly run
   His earthly course,—'Nay, Goody, let your text
Grow in the garden.—We have only one—
   Who knows that these dim eyes may see the next? 60
Summer will come again, and summer sun.
   And lilies too,—but I were sorely vext
To mar my garden, and cut short the blow
Of the last lily I may live to grow.'

'The last!' quoth she, 'and though the last it were—   65
   Lo! those two wantons, where they stand so proud
With waving plumes, and jewels in their hair,
   And painted cheeks, like Dagons to be bow'd
And curtsey'd to!—last Sabbath after pray'r,
   I heard the little Tomkins ask aloud   70
If they were angels—but I made him know
God's bright ones better, with a bitter blow!'

X

So speaking, they pursue the pebbly walk
   That leads to the white porch the Sunday throng,
Hand-coupled urchins in restrained talk,   75
   And anxious pedagogue that chastens wrong,
And posied churchwarden with solemn stalk,
   And gold-bedizen'd beadle flames along,
And gentle peasant clad in buff and green,
Like a meek cowslip in the spring serene;   80

And blushing maiden—modestly array'd
   In spotless white,—still conscious of the glass;
And she, the lonely widow, that hath made
   A sable covenant with grief,—alas!
She veils her tears under the deep, deep shade,   85
   While the poor kindly-hearted, as they pass,
Bend to unclouded childhood, and caress
Her boy,—so rosy!—and so fatherless!

XII

Thus, as good Christians ought, they all draw near
   The fair white temple to the timely call   90
Of pleasant bells that tremble in the ear.—
   Now the last frock, and scarlet hood, and shawl
Fade into dusk, in the dim atmosphere
   Of the low porch, and heav'n has won them all,
—Saving those two, that turn aside and pass   95
In velvet blossom, where all flesh is grass.

XIII

Ah me! to see their silken manors trail'd
   In purple luxuries—with restless gold,—
Flaunting the grass where widowhood has wail'd
   In blotted black,—over the heapy mould   100
Panting wave-wantonly! They never quail'd
   How the warm vanity abused the cold;
Nor saw the solemn faces of the gone
Sadly uplooking through transparent stone:

XIV

But swept their dwellings with unquiet light,   105
   Shocking the awful presence of the dead;
Where gracious natures would their eyes benight,
   Nor wear their being with a lip too red,
Nor move too rudely in the summer bright
   Of sun, but put staid sorrow in their tread,   110
Meting it into steps, with inward breath,
In very pity to bereaved death.

XV

Now in the church, time-sober'd minds reign
    To solemn pray'r, and the loud chaunted hymn,—
With glowing picturings of joys divine   115
    Painting the mistlight where the roof is dim;
But youth looks upward to the window shine,
    Warming with rose and purple and the swim
Of gold, as if thought-tinted by the stains
Of gorgeous light through many-colour'd panes;   120

XVI

Soiling the virgin snow wherein God hath
    Enrobed his angels,—and with absent eyes
Hearing of Heav'n, and its directed path,
    Thoughtful of slippers,—and the glorious skies
Clouding with satin,—till the preacher's wrath   125
    Consumes his pity, and he glows and cries,
With a deep voice that trembles in its might,
And earnest eyes grown eloquent in light:

XVII

'O that the vacant eye would learn to look
    On very beauty, and the heart embrace   130
True loveliness, and from this holy book
    Drink the warm-breathing tenderness and grace
Of love indeed! O that the young soul took
    Its virgin passion from the glorious face
Of fair religion, and address'd its strife,   135
To win the riches of eternal life!

XVIII

'Doth the vain heart love glory that is none,
   And the poor excellence of vain attire?
O go, and drown your eyes against the sun,
   The visible ruler of the starry quire,   140
Till boiling gold in giddy eddies run,
   Dazzling the brain with orbs of living fire;
And the faint soul down darkens into night,
And dies a burning martyrdom to light.

XIX

'O go, and gaze,—when the low winds of ev'n   145
   Breathe hymns, and Nature's many forests nod
Their gold-crown'd heads; and the rich blooms of heav'n
   Sun-ripen'd give their blushes up to God;
And mountain-rocks and cloudy steeps are riv'n
   By founts of fire, as smitten by the rod   150
Of heavenly Moses,—that your thirsty sense
May quench its longings of magnificence!

XX

'Yet suns shall perish—stars shall fade away—
   Day into darkness—darkness into death—
Death into silence; the warm light of day,   155
   The blooms of summer, the rich glowing breath
Of even—all shall wither and decay,
   Like the frail furniture of dreams beneath
The touch of morn—or bubbles of rich dyes
That break and vanish in the aching eyes.'   160

XXI

They hear, soul-blushing, and repentant shed
   Unwholesome thoughts in wholesome tears, and pour
Their sin to earth,—and with low drooping head
   Receive the solemn blessing, and implore
Its grace—then soberly with chasten'd tread,   165
   They meekly press towards the gusty door,
With humbled eyes that go to graze upon
The lowly grass—like him of Babylon.

The lowly grass!—O water-constant mind!
   Fast-ebbing holiness!—soon-fading grace   170
Of serious thought, as if the gushing wind
   Through the low porch had wash'd it from the face
For ever!—How they lift their eyes to find
   Old vanities.—Pride wins the very place
Of meekness, like a bird, and flutters now   175
With idle wings on the curl-conscious brow!

And lo! with eager looks they seek the way
   Of old temptation at the lowly gate;
To feast on feathers, and on vain array,
   And painted cheeks, and the rich glistering state   180
Of jewel-sprinkled locks.—But where are they,
   The graceless haughty ones that used to wait
With lofty neck, and nods, and stiffen'd eye?—
None challenge the old homage bending by.

In vain they look for the ungracious bloom   185
   Of rich apparel where it glow'd before,—
For Vanity has faded all to gloom,
   And lofty Pride has stiffen'd to the core,
For impious Life to tremble at its doom,—
   Set for a warning token evermore,   190
Whereon, as now, the giddy and the wise
Shall gaze with lifted hands and wond'ring eyes.

XXV

The aged priest goes on each sabbath morn,
   But shakes not sorrow under his grey hair;
The solemn clerk goes lavender'd and shorn,   195
   Nor stoops his back to the ungodly pair;—
And ancient lips that pucker'd up in scorn,
   Go smoothly breathing to the house of pray'r;
And in the garden-plot, from day to day,
The lily blooms its long white life away.   200

And where two haughty maidens use to be,
   In pride of plume, where plumy Death had trod,
Trailing their gorgeous velvets wantonly,
   Most unmeet pall, over the holy sod;—
There, gentle stranger, thou may'st only see   205
   Two sombre Peacocks.——Age, with sapient nod
Marking the spot, still tarries to declare
How they once lived, and wherefore they are there.

Song

I

The stars are with the voyager
    Wherever he may sail;
The moon is constant to her time;
    The sun will never fail;
But follow, follow round the world,   5
    The green earth and the sea;
So love is with the lover's heart,
    Wherever he may be.

II

Wherever he may be, the stars
    Must daily lose their light;   10
The moon will veil her in the shade;
    The sun will set at night.
The sun may set, but constant love
    Will shine when he's away;
So that dull night is never night,   15
    And day is brighter day.

Sonnet: To an Enthusiast

Young ardent soul, graced with fair Nature's truth,
Spring warmth of heart, and fervency of mind,
And still a large late love of all thy kind,
Spite of the world's cold practice and Time's tooth,—
For all these gifts, I know not, in fair sooth,   5

Whether to give thee joy, or bid thee blind
Thine eyes with tears,—that thou hast not resign'd
The passionate fire and freshness of thy youth:
For as the current of thy life shall flow,
Gilded by shine of sun or shadow stain'd,   10
Through flow'ry valley or unwholesome fen,
Thrice blessed in thy joy, or in thy woe
Thrice cursed of thy race,—thou art ordain'd
To share beyond the lot of common men.

Sonnet: It is not death

It is not death, that sometime in a sigh
This eloquent breath shall take its speechless flight;
That sometime these bright stars, that now reply
In sunlight to the sun, shall set in night;
That this warm conscious flesh shall perish quite,   5
And all life's ruddy springs forget to flow;
That thoughts shall cease, and the immortal spright
Be lapp'd in alien clay and laid below;
It is not death to know this,—but to know
That pious thoughts, which visit at new graves   10
In tender pilgrimage, will cease to go
So duly and so oft,—and when grass waves
Over the past-away, there may be then
No resurrection in the minds of men.

Silence

There is a silence where hath been no sound,
   There is a silence where no sound may be,
   In the cold grave—under the deep deep sea,
Or in wide desert where no life is found,
Which hath been mute, and still must sleep profound;   5
   No voice is hush'd—no life treads silently,
   But clouds and cloudy shadows wander free,
That never spoke, over the idle ground:
But in green ruins, in the desolate walls
   Of antique palaces, where Man hath been,   10
Though the dun fox, or wild hyena, calls,
   And owls, that flit continually between,
Shriek to the echo, and the low winds moan,
There the true Silence is, self-conscious and alone.

Sonnet to Vauxhall

'The English Garden'—Mason

The cold transparent ham is on my fork—
   It hardly rains—and hark the bell!—ding-dingle—
Away! Three thousand feet at gravel work,
   Mocking a Vauxhall shower!—Married and Single
Crush—rush;—Soak'd Silks with wet white Satin mingle.   5
   Hengler! Madame! round whom all bright sparks lurk,
Calls audibly on Mr. and Mrs. Pringle
   To study the Sublime, &c.—(vide Burke)

All Noses are upturn'd!—Whish—ish!—On high
   The rocket rushes—trails—just steals in sight—   10
Then droops and melts in bubbles of blue light—
   And Darkness reigns—Then balls flare up and die—
Wheels whiz—smack crackers—serpents twist—and then
   Back to the cold transparent ham again!

A Drop of Gin

Gin! Gin! a Drop of Gin!
What magnified Monsters circle therein!
   Ragged, and stained with filth and mud,
   Some plague-spotted, and some with blood!
Shapes of Misery, Shame, and Sin!   5
   Figures that make us loathe and tremble,
   Creatures scarce human that more resemble
Broods of diabolical kin,
Ghoule and Vampyre, Demon and Jin!

Gin! Gin! a Drop of Gin!   10
The dram of Satan! the liquor of Sin!—
   Distill'd from the fell
   Alembics of Hell,
By Guilt and Death, his own brother and twin!
   That man might fall   15
   Still lower than all
The meanest creatures with scale and fin.
But hold—we are neither Barebones nor Prynne,
   Who lash'd with such rage
   The sins of the age;   20
Then, instead of making too much of din,
   Let Anger be mute,
   And sweet Mercy dilute,
With a drop of Pity, the Drop of Gin!

Gin! Gin! a Drop of Gin!—   25
When darkly Adversity's day's set in,
    And the friends and peers
    Of earlier years
Prove warm without, but cold within,—
    And cannot retrace   30
    A familiar face
That's steep'd in poverty up to the chin;—
But snub, neglect, cold-shoulder, and cut
The ragged pauper, misfortune's butt,
Hardly acknowledg'd by kith and kin,   35
    Because, poor rat!
    He has no cravat;
A seedy coat, and a hole in that!—
No sole to his shoe, and no brim to his hat;
Nor a change of linen—except his skin;—   40
    No gloves—no vest,
    Either second or best;
And what is worse than all the rest,
No light heart, tho' his breeches are thin,—
    While Time elopes   45
    With all golden hopes,
And even with those of pewter and tin,—
    The brightest dreams,
    And the best of schemes,
All knocked down, like a wicket by Mynn,—   50
    Each castle in air
    Seized by Giant Despair,
No prospect in life worth a minikin pin,—
    No credit—no cash,
    No cold mutton to hash,   55
    No bread—not even potatoes to mash;
No coal in the cellar, no wine in the binn,—
    Smash'd, broken to bits,
    With judgments and writs,

Bonds, bills, and cognovits distracting the wits,   60
In the webs that the spiders of Chancery spin,—
    Till weary of life, its worry and strife,
    Black visions are rife of a razor, a knife,
Of poison—a rope—'louping over a linn.'—
Gin! Gin! a Drop of Gin!   65
Oh! then its tremendous temptations begin,
    To take, alas!
    To the fatal glass,—
And happy the wretch that it does not win
    To change the black hue   70
    Of his ruin to blue—
While Angels sorrow, and Demons grin—
    And lose the rheumatic
    Chill of his attic
By plunging into the Palace of Gin!   75

The Song of the Shirt

With fingers weary and worn,
    With eyelids heavy and red,
A Woman sat, in unwomanly rags,
    Plying her needle and thread—
        Stitch! stitch! stitch!   5
In poverty, hunger, and dirt,
And still with a voice of dolorous pitch
She sang the 'Song of the Shirt!'

'Work! work! work!
While the cock is crowing aloof!   10
    And work—work—work,
Till the stars shine through the roof!
It's O! to be a slave
    Along with the barbarous Turk,
Where woman has never a soul to save,   15
    If this is Christian work!

'Work—work—work
Till the brain begins to swim;
    Work—work—work
Till the eyes are heavy and dim!   20
Seam, and gusset, and band,
    Band, and gusset, and seam,
Till over the buttons I fall asleep,
    And sew them on in a dream!

'O! Men with Sisters dear!   25
    O! Men! with Mothers and Wives!
It is not linen you're wearing out,
    But human creatures' lives!
        Stitch—stitch—stitch,
    In poverty, hunger, and dirt,   30
Sewing at once, with a double thread,
    A Shroud as well as a Shirt.

'But why do I talk of Death?
    That Phantom of grisly bone,
I hardly fear his terrible shape,   35
    It seems so like my own—
    It seems so like my own,
    Because of the fasts I keep,
Oh! God! that bread should be so dear,
    And flesh and blood so cheap!   40

'Work—work—work!
  My labour never flags;
And what are its wages? A bed of straw,
  A crust of bread—and rags.
That shatter'd roof,—and this naked floor—   45
  A table—a broken chair—
And a wall so blank, my shadow I thank
  For sometimes falling there!

'Work—work—work!
From weary chime to chime,   50
  Work—work—work—
As prisoners work for crime!
  Band, and gusset, and seam,
  Seam, and gusset, and band,
Till the heart is sick, and the brain benumb'd,   55
  As well as the weary hand.

'Work—work—work,
In the dull December light,
  And work—work—work,
When the weather is warm and bright—   60
While underneath the eaves
  The brooding swallows cling
As if to show me their sunny backs
  And twit me with the spring.

'Oh! but to breathe the breath   65
Of the cowslip and primrose sweet—
  With the sky above my head,
And the grass beneath my feet,
For only one short hour
  To feel as I used to feel,   70
Before I knew the woes of want
  And the walk that costs a meal!

'Oh but for one short hour!
  A respite however brief!
No blessed leisure for Love or Hope,   75
  But only time for Grief!
A little weeping would ease my heart,
  But in their briny bed
My tears must stop, for every drop
  Hinders needle and thread!'   80

Seam, and gusset, and band,
Band, and gusset, and seam,
    Work, work, work,
Like the Engine that works by Steam!
A mere machine of iron and wood   85
    That toils for Mammon's sake—
Without a brain to ponder and craze
    Or a heart to feel—and break!

With fingers weary and worn,
  With eyelids heavy and red,   90
A Woman sate in unwomanly rags,
  Plying her needle and thread—
    Stitch! stitch! stitch!
  In poverty, hunger, and dirt,
And still with a voice of dolorous pitch   95
Would that its tone could reach the Rich!—
  She sang this 'Song of the Shirt!'

The Bridge of Sighs

'Drown'd! drown'd!'—*Hamlet*

One more Unfortunate,
Weary of breath,
Rashly importunate,
Gone to her death!

Take her up tenderly,   5
Lift her with care;
Fashion'd so slenderly,
Young, and so fair!

Look at her garments
Clinging like cerements;   10
Whilst the wave constantly
Drips from her clothing;
Take her up instantly,
Loving, not loathing.—

Touch her not scornfully;   15
Think of her mournfully,
Gently and humanly;
Not of the stains of her,
All that remains of her
Now is pure womanly.   20

Make no deep scrutiny
Into her mutiny
Rash and undutiful:
Past all dishonour
Death has left on her   25
Only the beautiful.

Still, for all slips of hers,
One of Eve's family—
Wipe those poor lips of hers
Oozing so clammily.   30

Loop up her tresses
Escaped from the comb,
Her fair auburn tresses;
Whilst wonderment guesses   35
Where was her home?

Who was her father?
Who was her mother?
Had she a sister?
Had she a brother?
Or was there a dearer one   40
Still, and a nearer one
Yet, than all other?

Alas! for the rarity
Of Christian charity
Under the sun!   45
Oh! it was pitiful!
Near a whole city full,
Home she had none!

Sisterly, brotherly,
Fatherly, motherly,   50
Feelings had changed:
Love, by harsh evidence,
Thrown from its eminence;
Even God's providence
Seeming estranged.   55

Where the lamps quiver
So far in the river,
With many a light
From window and casement,
From garret to basement,   60
She stood, with amazement,
Houseless by night.

The bleak wind of March
Made her tremble and shiver;
But not the dark arch,   65
Or the black flowing river;
Mad from life's history,
Glad to death's mystery,
Swift to be hurl'd—
Anywhere, anywhere,   70
Out of the world!

In she plunged boldly,
No matter how coldly
The rough river ran,—
Over the brink of it,   75
Picture it—think of it,
Dissolute man!
Lave in it, drink of it,
Then, if you can!

Take her up tenderly,   80
Lift her with care;
Fashion'd so slenderly,
Young, and so fair!

Ere her limbs frigidly
Stiffen too rigidly,   85
Decently,—kindly,—

Smoothe and compose them:
And her eyes, close them,
Staring so blindly!

Dreadfully staring   90
Thro' muddy impurity,
As when with the daring
Last look of despairing,
Fix'd on futurity.

Perishing gloomily,   95
Spurr'd by contumely,
Cold inhumanity,
Burning insanity,
Into her rest.—
Cross her hands humbly,   100
As if praying dumbly,
Over her breast!

Owning her weakness,
Her evil behaviour,
And leaving, with meekness,   105
Her sins to her Saviour!

Stanzas

Farewell, Life! My senses swim;
And the world is growing dim;
Thronging shadows cloud the light,
Like the advent of the night,—
Colder, colder, colder still   5
Upward steals a vapour chill—

Strong the earthly odour grows—
I smell the Mould above the Rose!
Welcome, Life! the Spirit strives!
Strength returns, and hope revives;   10
Cloudy fears and shapes forlorn
Fly like shadows at the morn,—
O'er the earth there comes a bloom—
Sunny light for sullen gloom,
Warm perfume for vapour cold—   15
I smell the Rose above the Mould!

Lear

A poor old king, with sorrow for my crown,
Throned upon straw, and mantled with the wind—
For pity, my own tears have made me blind
That I might never see my children's frown;
And, may be, madness, like a friend, has thrown   5
A folded fillet over my dark mind,
So that unkindly speech may sound for kind—
Albeit I know not.—I am childish grown—
And have not gold to purchase wit withal—
I that have once maintain'd most royal state—   10
A very bankrupt now that may not call
My child, my child—all beggar'd save in tears,
Wherewith I daily weep an old man's fate,
Foolish—and blind—and overcome with years!

Stanzas

Is there a bitter pang for love removed,
　　O God! The dead love doth not cost more tears
Than the alive, the loving, the beloved—
　　Not yet, not yet beyond all hopes and fears!
　　　　Would I were laid　　　　　　　　　　　　5
　　　　Under the shade
Of the calm grave, and the long grass of years,—

That love might die with sorrow:—I am sorrow;
　　And she, that loves me tenderest, doth press
Most poison from my cruel lips, and borrow　　　　10
　　Only new anguish from the old caress;
　　　　Oh, this world's grief
　　　　Hath no relief
In being wrung from a great happiness.

Would I had never filled thine eyes with love,　　15
　　For love is only tears: would I had never
Breathed such a curse-like blessing as we prove;
　　Now, if 'Farewell' *could* bless thee, I would sever!
　　　　Would I were laid
　　　　Under the shade　　　　　　　　　　　　20
Of the cold tomb, and the long grass for ever!

Ode on a Distant Prospect of Clapham Academy[1]

Ah me! those old familiar bounds!
That classic house, those classic grounds,
  My pensive thought recalls!
What tender urchins now confine,
What little captives now repine,   5
  Within yon irksome walls?

Ay, that's the very house! I know
Its ugly windows, ten a-row!
  Its chimneys in the rear!
And there's the iron rod so high,   10
That drew the thunder from the sky,
  And turn'd our table-beer!

There I was birch'd! there I was bred!
There like a little Adam fed
  From Learning's woeful tree!   15
The weary tasks I used to con!—
The hopeless leaves I wept upon!—
  Most fruitless leaves to me!—

The summon'd class!—the awful bow!—
I wonder who is master now   20
  And wholesome anguish sheds!
How many ushers now employs,
How many maids to see the boys
  Have nothing in their heads!

[1] No connexion with any other ode.

And Mrs. S***?—Doth she abet 25
(Like Pallas in the parlour) yet
   Some favour'd two or three,—
The little Crichtons of the hour,
Her muffin-medals that devour,
   And swill her prize—bohea? 30

Ay, there's the play-ground! there's the lime
Beneath whose shade in summer's prime
   So wildly I have read!—
Who sits there *now*, and skims the cream
Of young Romance, and weaves a dream 35
   Of Love and Cottage-bread?

Who struts the Randall of the walk?
Who models tiny heads in chalk?
   Who scoops the light canoe?
What early genius buds apace? 40
Where's Poynter? Harris? Bowers? Chase?
   Hal Baylis? blithe Carew?

Alack! they're gone—a thousand ways!
And some are serving in 'the Greys,'
   And some have perish'd young!— 45
Jack Harris weds his second wife;
Hal Baylis drives the *wane* of life;
   And blithe Carew—is hung!

Grave Bowers teaches A B C
To savages at Owhyee; 50
   Poor Chase is with the worms!—
All, all are gone—the olden breed!—
New crops of mushroom boys succeed,
   'And push us from our *forms!*'

Lo! where they scramble forth, and shout,   55
And leap, and skip, and mob about,
    At play where we have play'd!
Some hop, some run (some fall), some twine
Their crony arms; some in the shine,
    And some are in the shade!   60

Lo! there what mix'd conditions run!
The orphan lad; the widow's son;
    And Fortune's favour'd care—
The wealthy-born, for whom she hath
Mac-Adamized the future path—   65
    The Nabob's pamper'd heir!

Some brightly starr'd—some evil born,—
For honour some, and some for scorn,—
    For fair or foul renown!
Good, bad, indifferent—none may lack!   70
Look, here's a White, and there's a Black!
    And there's a Creole brown!

Some laugh and sing, some mope and weep,
And wish *their* frugal sires would keep
    Their only sons at home;—   75
Some tease the future tense, and plan
The full-grown doings of the man,
    And pant for years to come!

A foolish wish! There's one at hoop;
And four at *fives!* and five who stoop   80
    The marble taw to speed!
And one that curvets in and out,
Reining his fellow Cob about,—
    Would I were in his *steed!*

77

Yet he would gladly halt and drop   85
That boyish harness off, to swop
  With this world's heavy van—
To toil, to tug. O little fool!
While thou canst be a horse at school
  To wish to be a man!   90

Perchance thou deem'st it were a thing
To wear a crown,—to be a king!
  And sleep on regal down!
Alas! thou know'st not kingly cares;
Far happier is thy head that wears   95
  That hat without a crown!

And dost thou think that years acquire
New added joys? Dost think thy sire
  More happy than his son?
That manhood's mirth?—Oh, go thy ways   100
To Drury Lane when——*plays*,
  And see how *forced* our fun!

Thy taws are brave!—thy tops are rare!—
Our tops are spun with coils of care,
  Our *dumps* are no delight!—   105
The Elgin marbles are but tame
And 'tis at best a sorry game
  To fly the Muse's kite!

Our hearts are dough, our heels are lead,
Our topmost joys fall dull and dead   110
  Like balls with no rebound!
And often with a faded eye
We look behind, and send a sigh
  Towards that merry ground!

Then be contented. Thou hast got—   115
  The most of heaven in thy young lot
    There's sky-blue in thy cup!
  Thou'lt find thy Manhood all too fast—
  Soon come, soon gone! and Age at last
    A sorry *breaking-up!*   120

Epigram: The Superiority of Machinery

A Mechanic his labour will often discard
  If the rate of his pay he dislikes;
But a clock—and its *case* is uncommonly hard—
  Will continue to work though it *strikes.*

Bailey Ballad No. II

'Love with a witness!'

He has shav'd off his whiskers and blacken'd his brows,
Wears a patch and a wig of false hair,—
But it's him—Oh it's him!—we exchanged lovers' vows
When I lived up in Cavendish Square.

He had beautiful eyes, and his lips were the same,   5
And his voice was as soft as a flute—
Like a Lord or a Marquis he look'd, when he came
To make love in his master's best suit.

If I lived for a thousand long years from my birth,
I shall never forget what he told;   10
How he lov'd me beyond the rich women of earth,
With their jewels and silver and gold!

When he kiss'd me, and bade me adieu with a sigh,
By the light of the sweetest of moons,
Oh how little I dreamt I was bidding good-bye   15
To my Missis's tea-pot and spoons!

Mary's Ghost

A Pathetic Ballad

1

'Twas in the middle of the night,
    To sleep young William tried,
When Mary's ghost came stealing in,
    And stood at his bed-side.

2

O William dear! O William dear!   5
    My rest eternal ceases;
Alas! my everlasting peace
    Is broken into pieces.

3

I thought the last of all my cares
    Would end with my last minute;   10
But tho' I went to my long home,
    I didn't stay long in it.

4

The body-snatchers they have come,
    And made a snatch at me;
It's very hard them kind of men   15
    Won't let a body be!

5

You thought that I was buried deep
   Quite decent like and chary,
But from her grave in Mary-bone
   They've come and boned your Mary.   20

6

The arm that used to take your arm
   Is took to Dr. Vyse;
And both my legs are gone to walk
   The hospital at Guy's.

7

I vow'd that you should have my hand,   25
   But fate gives us denial;
You'll find it there, at Dr. Bell's
   In spirits and a phial.

8

As for my feet, the little feet
   You used to call so pretty,   30
There's one, I know, in Bedford Row,
   The t'other's in the city.

9

I can't tell where my head is gone,
   But Doctor Carpue can:
As for my trunk, it's all pack'd up   35
   To go by Pickford's van.

10

I wish you'd go to Mr. P.
   And save me such a ride;
I don't half like the outside place,
   They've took for my inside.   40

11

The cock it crows—I must begone!
   My William we must part!
But I'll be yours in death, altho'
   Sir Astley has my heart.

12

Don't go to weep upon my grave,   45
   And think that there I be;
They haven't left an atom there
   Of my anatomie.

Faithless Nelly Gray

A Pathetic Ballad

Ben Battle was a soldier bold,
   And used to war's alarms:
But a cannon-ball took off his legs,
   So he laid down his arms!

Now as they bore him off the field,   5
   Said he, 'Let others shoot,
For here I leave my second leg,
   And the Forty-second Foot!'

The army-surgeons made him limbs:
   Said he,—'They're only pegs: 10
But there's as wooden members quite
   As represent my legs!'

Now Ben he loved a pretty maid,
   Her name was Nelly Gray;
So he went to pay her his devours   15
   When he'd devoured his pay!

But when he called on Nelly Gray,
   She made him quite a scoff;
And when she saw his wooden legs,
   Began to take them off!   20

'O, Nelly Gray! O, Nelly Gray!
   Is this your love so warm?
The love that loves a scarlet coat
   Should be more uniform!'

Said she, 'I loved a soldier once,   25
   For he was blythe and brave;
But I will never have a man
   With both legs in the grave!

'Before you had those timber toes,
   Your love I did allow,   30
But then, you know, you stand upon
   Another footing now!'

'O, Nelly Gray! O, Nelly Gray!
   For all your jeering speeches,
At duty's call, I left my legs   35
   In Badajos's *breaches!*'

'Why, then,' said she, 'you've lost the feet
   Of legs in war's alarms,
And now you cannot wear your shoes
   Upon your feats of arms!'   40

'O, false and fickle Nelly Gray;
    I know why you refuse:—
Though I've no feet—some other man
    Is standing in my shoes!

'I wish I ne'er had seen your face;   45
    But, now, a long farewell!
For you will be my death;—alas!
    You will not be my *Nell!*'

Now when he went from Nelly Gray,
    His heart so heavy got—   50
And life was such a burthen grown,
    It made him take a knot!

So round his melancholy neck,
    A rope he did entwine,
And, for his second time in life,   55
    Enlisted in the Line!

One end he tied around a beam,
    And then removed his pegs,
And, as his legs were off,—of course,
    He soon was off his legs!   60

And there he hung, till he was dead
    As any nail in town,—
For though distress had cut him up,
    It could not cut him down!

A dozen men sat on his corpse,   65
    To find out why he died—
And they buried Ben in four crossroads,
    With a *stake* in his inside!

THOMAS LOVELL BEDDOES

The Phantom-Wooer

I

A Ghost, that loved a lady fair,
Ever in the starry air
   Of midnight at her pillow stood;
And, with a sweetness skies above
The luring words of human love,   5
   Her soul the phantom wooed.
Sweet and sweet is their poisoned note,
The little snakes of silver throat,
In mossy skulls that nest and lie,
Ever singing 'die, oh! die.'   10

II

Young soul put off your flesh, and come
With me into the quiet tomb,
   Our bed is lovely, dark, and sweet;
The earth will swing us, as she goes,
Beneath our coverlid of snows,   15
   And the warm leaden sheet.
Dear and dear is their poisoned note,
The little snakes of silver throat,
In mossy skulls that nest and lie,
Ever singing 'die, oh! die.'   20

Pygmalion

The Cyprian Statuary

There stood a city along Cyprus' side
Lavish of palaces, an arched tide
Of unrolled rocks; and where the deities dwelled
Their clustered domes pushed up the noon and swelled
With the emotion of the god within,   5
As doth earth's hemisphere, when showers begin
To tickle the still spirit at its core
Till pastures tremble and the river-shore
Squeezes out buds at every dewy pore;
And there were pillars, from some mountain's heart,   10
Thronging beneath a wide imperial floor
That bent with riches; and there stood apart
A palace oft accompanied by trees
That laid their shadows in the galleries
Under the coming of the endless light,   15
Net-like; who trod the marble night or day,
By moon, or lamp or sunless day-shine white,
Would brush the shaking ghostly leaves away
Which might be tendrils or a knot of wine,
Burst from the depth of a faint window vine,   20
With a bird pecking it—and round the hall
And wandering stair-case, within every wall
Of sea-ward portico, and sleeping chamber,
Whose patient lamp distilled a day of amber,
There stood and sate or made rough steeds their throne   25
Immortal generations wrung from stone
Alike too beautiful for life and death
And bodies that a soul of mortal breath
Would be the dross of.
                          Such a house as this

Within a garden hard by Salamis, 30
(Cyprus's city-crown and capital
Ere Paphos was, and at whose ocean-wall
Beauty and love's paternal waves do beat
That sprouted Venus:) such a fair retreat
Lonely Pygmalion self inhabited 35
Whose fiery chisel with creation fed
The shipwrecked rocks; who paid the heavens again
Diamonds for ice; who made gods who make men.
Lonely Pygmalion: you might see him go
Along the streets where markets thickest flow 40
Doubling his gown across his thinking breast
And the men fall aside; nor only pressed
Out of his elbows' way but left a place
A sun-room for him that his mind had space
And none went near; none in his sweep would venture 45
For you might feel that he was but the centre
Of an inspired round, the middle spark
Of a great moon setting aside the dark
And cloudy people. As he went along
The chambered ladies silenced the half-song 50
And let the wheel unheeded whirl and skim
To get their eyes blest by the sight of him.
So locks were swept from every eye that drew
Sun for the soul through circles violet-blue
Mild brown or passionate black.
                           Still, discontent, 55
Over his sensual kind the sculptor went
Walking his thoughts. Yet Cyprus' girls be fair;
Daybright and evening-soft the maidens are
And witching like the midnight and their pleasure
Silent and deep as midnight's starry treasure. 60
Lovely and young, Pygmalion yet loved none.
His soul was bright and lonely as the sun
Like which he could create—and in its might

There lived another Spirit wild and bright
That came and went; and when it came, its light   65
On these dim earthy things, turn where he will,
Its light, shape, beauty were reflected still.
Daytime and dark it came—like a dim mist
Shelling a god it rolled, and ere he wist
It fell aside, and dawned a shape of grace   70
And an inspired and melancholy face
Whose lips were smile-buds dewy—into him
It rolled like sunlight, till his sight was dim
And it was in his heart and soul again,
Not seen but breathed.
                              There was a grassy plain   75
A pasture of the deer, Olympus' mountain
Was the plain's night, the picture of its fountain;
Unto which unfrequented dell and wood
Unwittingly his solitary mood
Oft drew him. In the water lay   80
A fragment of pale marble, which they say
Slipped from some fissure in the agued moon
Which had caught earth-quake and a deadly swoon
When the sun touched her with his hilly shade.
Weeds grew upon it and the streamlet made   85
A wanton music with its ragged side
And birds had nests there. One still eventide
When they were perched and sleeping passed this man
Startling the air with thoughts which over-ran
The compass of his mind; writing the sand   90
Idly he paused and laid unwitting hand
On the cold stone. How smooth the touch! It felt
Less porous than a lip which kisses melt
And diamond-hard. That night his workmen wrought
With iron under it and it was brought,   95
This dripping quarry while the sky was starry
Home to the weary yearning statuary.

He saw no sky that day, no dark that night
For through the hours his lamp was full of light,
Shadowing the pavement with his busy right;   100
Day after day they saw not in the street
The wondrous artist, some immortal feat
Absorbed him. And yet often in the noon
When the town slept beneath the sweltering June
—The rich within; the poor man on the stair—   105
He stole unseen into the meadow's air
And fed on sight of summer—till the life
Was too abundant in him and so rife
With light creative he went in alone
And poured it warm upon the growing stone.   110
The magic chisel thrust and gashed and swept
Flying and manifold; no cloud e'er wept
So fast, so thick, so light upon the close
Of shapeless green it meant to make a rose—
And as insensibly out of a stick   115
Dead in the winter-time, the dew-drops quick
And the thin sun-beams and the airy shower
Raise and unwrap a many-leaved flower
And then a fruit—So from the barren stock
Of the deer-shading formless valley-rock,   120
This close stone-bud, he, quiet as the air,
Had shaped a lady wonderfully fair.
Dear to the eyes—a delicate delight
For all her marble symmetry was white
As brow and bosom should be; save some azure   125
Which waited for a loving lip's erasure
Upon her shoulder to be turned to blush.
And she was smooth and full, as if one gush
Of life had washed her, or as if a sleep
Lay on her eyelid easier to sweep   130
Than bee from daisy. Who could help a sigh
At seeing a beauty stand so life-lessly

But that it was too beautiful to die?
Dealer of immortality
Greater than Jove himself, for only he   135
Can such eternize as the grave has ta'en
And open heaven by the gate of pain;
What art thou now, divine Pygmalion?
Divine! gods counting human. Thou hast done
That glory which has undone thee for ever,   140
For thou art weak and tearful and dost shiver
Wintrily sad and thy life's healthy river,
With which thy body once was overflown,
Is dried and sunken to its banks of bone.

   He carved it not; nor was the chisel's play   145
That dashed the earthen hindrances away
Driven and diverted by his muscle's sway;
The winged tool as digging out a spell
Followed a magnet, wheresoe'er it fell,
That sucked and led it right—and for the rest   150
The living form with which the stone be blest
Was the loved image stepping from his breast.
And therefore loves he it and therefore stays
About the she-rock's feet, from hour to hour,
Anchored to her by his own heart; the power   155
Of the isle's Venus therefore doth he pray—
'Goddess that made me, save thy son, and save
The man that made thee, goddess, from the grave.
Thou know'st it not; it is a fearful coop
Dark, cold, and horrible—a blinded loop   160
In Pluto's madhouse' green and wormy wall.
O save me from 't; let me not die, like all,
For I am but like one—not yet, not yet,
At least not yet—and why? my eyes are wet
With the thick dregs of immature despair,   165
With bitter blood out of my empty heart,
I breathe not aught but my own sighs for air,

And my life's strongest is a dying start.
No sour grief there is to me unwed,
I could not be more lifeless being dead. 170
Then let me die—Ha did she pity me?
Oh she can never love—did you not see,
How still she bears the music of my moan?
Her heart? Ah touch it.—Fool. I love the stone.
Inspire her, gods—Oft ye have wasted life 175
On the deformed, the hideous and the vile:
Oh grant it my sweet rock—my only wife.
I do not ask it long: a little while—
A year—a day—an hour let it be!
For that I'll give you my eternity 180
Or let it be a fiend if ye will send
Something yon form to humanize and bend,
Within those limbs, and when the new-poured blood
Flows in such veins the worst must soon be good.
They will not hear.—Thou Jove—or thou, Apollo, 185
Aye—thou—thou know'st—Oh listen to my groan.
'Twas Niobe thou drovest from flesh to stone,
Shew this the hole she broke, and let her follow
That mother's track of steps and eyelid rain
Treading them backwards into life again. 190
Life said I? lives she not? is there not gone
My life into her which I pasture on,
Dead where she is not? Live, thou statue fair,
Live, thou dear marble! or shall go wild.
I cover thee my sweet, I leave thee there 195
Behind this curtain, my delicious child,
That they may secretly begin to give
My prayer to thee—when I return, oh live!
Oh live—or I live not.'—And so he went,
Leaving the statue in its darksome tent. 200
    Morn after morn sadder the artist came,
His prayer, his disappointment were the same.

But when he gazed she was more near to woman;
There was a fleshy pink—a dimple wrought
That trembled—and the cheek was growing human   205
With the flushed distance of a rising thought
That still crept nearer. Yet no further sign!
And now, Pygmalion, that weak life of thine
Shakes like a dew-drop in a broken rose—
Or incense parting from the altar glows.   210
'Tis the last look and he is made no more:
By rule and figure he could prove at large
She never can be born, and from the shore
His foot is stretching into Charon's barge.
Upon the pavement ghastly is he lying   215
Cold with the last and stoniest embrace,
Elysium's light illumines all his face,
His eyes have a wild starry grace
Of heaven, into whose depth of depths he's dying
   A sound, with which the air doth shake   220
Extinguishing the window of moonlight.
A pang of music dropping round delight,
As if sweet music's honiest heart did break.
Such a flash and such a sound the world
Is stung by as if something was unfurled   225
That held great bliss within its inmost curled.
Roof after roof the palace rends asunder,
And then—a sight of joy and placid wonder!—
He lies beside a fountain on the knee
Of the sweet woman-statue, quietly   230
Weeping the tears of his felicity.

Letter to B. W. Procter

From Göttingen; March, 1826

To-day a truant from the odd old bones
And winds of flesh, which, as tamed rocks and stones
Piled cavernously make his body's dwelling,
Have housed man's soul: there, where time's billows swelling
Make a deep ghostly and invisible sea   5
Of melted worlds antediluvially
Upon the sand of ever-crumbling hours,
God-founded, stands the castle, all its towers
With veiny tendrils ivied: this bright day
I leave its chambers and with oars away   10
Seek some enchanted island where to play.
And what do you, that in the enchantment dwell
And should be raving ever, a wild swell
Of passionate life rolling about the world,
Now sun-sucked to the clouds, dashed on the curled   15
Leaf-hidden daisies; an incarnate storm
Letting the sun through on the meadows yellow;
Or anything except that earthy fellow
That wise dog's brother, man? O shame to tell!
Make tea in Circe's cup, boil the cool well,   20
The well Pierian, which no bird dare sip
But nightingales. There let kettles dip
Who write their simpering sonnets to its song,
And walk on Sundays in Parnassus' park:
Take thy example from the sunny lark,   25
Throw off the mantle which conceals the soul,
The many-citied world, and seek thy goal
Straight as a starbeam falls. Creep not nor climb
As they who place their topmost of sublime
On some peak of this planet pitifully;   30

Dart eaglewise with open wings and fly,
Until you meet the gods. Thus counsel I
The men who can, but tremble to be great;
Cursed be the fool who taught to hesitate
And to regret: time lost most bitterly.   35
And thus I write and I dare write to thee,
Fearing that still, as you were wont to do,
You feed and fear some asinine Review.
Let Jaggernaut roll on, and we, whose sires
Blooded his wheels and prayed around his fires,   40
Laugh at the leaden ass in the god's skin.
Example follows precept: I have been
Giving some negro minutes of the night
Freed from the slavery of my ruling spright
Anatomy the grim, to a new story   45
In whose satiric pathos we will glory.
In it Despair has married wildest Mirth
And to their wedding-banquet all the earth
Is bade to bring its enmities and loves
Triumphs and horrors: you shall see the doves   50
Billing with quiet joy and all the while
Their nest's the scull of some old king of Nile:
But he who fills the cups and makes the jest
Pipes to the dancers, is the fool o' the feast.
Who's he? I've dug him up and decked him trim   55
And made a mock, a fool, a slave of him
Who was the planet's tyrant: dotard Death:
Man's hate and dread: not with a stoical breath
To meet him like Augustus standing up,
Nor with grave saws to season the cold cup   60
Like the philosopher, nor yet to hail
His coming with a verse or jesting tale
As Adrian did and More: but of his night,
His moony ghostliness and silent might
To rob him, to uncypress him i' the light   65

To unmask all his secrets; make him play
Momus o'er wine by torchlight is the way
To conquer him and kill; and from the day
Spurned, hissed and hooted send him back again
An unmask'd braggart to his bankrupt den.   70
For death is more 'a jest' than Life, you see
Contempt grows quick from familiarity.
I owe this wisdom to Anatomy.—
Your Muse is younger in her soul than mine:
O feed her still on woman's smiles and wine   75
And give the world a tender song once more,
For all the good can love and can adore
What's human, fair and gentle. Few, I know,
Can bear to sit at my board when I show
The wretchedness and folly of man's all   80
And laugh myself right heartily. Your call
Is higher and more human: I will do
Unsociably my part and still be true
To my own soul: but e'er admire you
And own that you have nature's kindest trust   85
Her weak and dear to nourish, that I must.
Then fare, as you deserve it, well, and live
In the calm feelings you to others give.

The Ghost's Moonshine

I

It is midnight, my wedded;
    Let us lie under
The tempest bright, my dreaded,
    In the warm thunder:

Tremble and weep not! What can you fear?
    My heart's best wish is thine,—
That thou wert white, and bedded
    On the softest bier,
      In the ghosts' moonshine.
    Is that the wind? No, no;
    Only two devils, that blow
    Through the murderer's ribs to and fro,
      In the ghosts' moonshine.

II

    Who is there, she said afraid, yet
      Stirring and awaking   15
    The poor old dead? His spade, it
      Is only making—
(Tremble and weep not! What do you crave?)
      Where yonder grasses twine,
A pleasant bed, my maid, that   20
    Children call a grave,
      In the cold moonshine.
    Is that the wind? No, no;
    Only two devils, that blow
    Through the murderer's ribs to and fro,   25
      In the ghosts' moonshine.

III

    What dost thou strain above her
      Lovely throat's whiteness?
    A silken chain, to cover
      Her bosom's brightness?   30
Tremble and weep not: what dost thou fear?
    —My blood is spilt like wine,
    Thou hast strangled and slain me, lover,

Thou hast stabbed me, dear,
  In the ghosts' moonshine.   35
Is that the wind? No, no;
Only her goblin doth blow
Through the murderer's ribs to and fro,
  In its own moonshine.

Dirge: *If thou wilt ease thine heart*

If thou wilt ease thine heart
Of love and all its smart,
    Then sleep, dear, sleep;
And not a sorrow
  Hang any tear on your eyelashes;   5
    Lie still and deep,
  Sad soul, until the sea-wave washes
The rim o' th' sun to-morrow,
    In eastern sky.

But wilt thou cure thy heart   10
Of love and all its smart,
    Then die, dear, die;
'Tis deeper, sweeter,
  Than on a rose bank to lie dreaming
    With folded eye;   15
  And then alone, amid the beaming
Of love's stars, thou'lt meet her
    In eastern sky.

Song: Squats on a toad-stool

Squats on a toad-stool under a tree
  A bodiless childfull of life in the gloom,
Crying with frog voice, 'What shall I be?
Poor unborn ghost, for my mother killed me
  Scarcely alive in her wicked womb.   5
What shall I be? shall I creep to the egg
  That's cracking asunder yonder by Nile,
    And with eighteen toes,
    And a snuff-taking nose,
  Make an Egyptian crocodile?   10
  Sing, "Catch a mummy by the leg
  And crunch him with an upper jaw,
  Wagging tail and clenching claw;
  Take a bill-full from my craw,
  Neighbour raven, caw, O caw,   15
  Grunt, my crocky, pretty maw!"

'Swine, shall I be one? 'Tis a dear dog;
  But for a smile, and kiss, and pout,
  I much prefer *your* black-lipped snout,
    Little, gruntless, fairy hog,   20
    Godson of the hawthorn hedge.
  For, when Ringwood snuffs me out,
    And 'gins my tender paunch to grapple,
    Sing, " 'Twixt your ancles visage wedge,
      And roll up like an apple."   25

'Serpent Lucifer, how do you do?
Of your worms and your snakes I'd be one or two
  For in this dear planet of wool and of leather
'Tis pleasant to need no shirt, breeches or shoe,

And have arm, leg, and belly together.   30
Then aches your head, or are you lazy?
Sing, "Round your neck your belly wrap,
Tail-a-top, and make your cap
    Any bee and daisy."

'I'll not be a fool, like the nightingale   35
Who sits up all midnight without any ale,
    Making a noise with his nose;
Nor a camel, although 'tis a beautiful back;
Nor a duck, notwithstanding the music of quack
    And the webby, mud-patting toes.   40
I'll be a new bird with the head of an ass,
    Two pigs' feet, two men's feet, and two of a hen;
Devil-winged; dragon-bellied; grave-jawed, because grass
    Is a beard that's soon shaved, and grows seldom again
      Before it is summer; so cow all the rest;   45
      The new Dodo is finished. O! come to my nest.'

Song: *A cypress-bough, and a rose-wreath sweet*

    A cypress-bough, and a rose-wreath sweet,
    A wedding-robe, and a winding-sheet,
      A bridal-bed and a bier.
     Thine be the kisses, maid,
      And smiling Love's alarms;   5
    And thou, pale youth, be laid
      In the grave's cold arms.
     Each in his own charms,
       Death and Hymen both are here;
       So up with scythe and torch,   10
       And to the old church porch,
      While all the bells ring clear:

And rosy, rosy the bed shall bloom,
And earthy, earthy heap up the tomb.

Now tremble dimples on your cheek,   15
Sweet be your lips to taste and speak,
    For he who kisses is near:
For her the bridegroom fair,
    In youthful power and force;
For him the grizard bare,   20
    Pale knight on a pale horse,
    To woo him to a corpse.
      Death and Hymen both are here;
      So up with scythe and torch,
      And to the old church porch,   25
     While all the bells ring clear:
And rosy, rosy the bed shall bloom,
And earthy, earthy heap up the tomb.

Song: Old Adam, the carrion crow

Old Adam, the carrion crow,
    The old crow of Cairo;
He sat in the shower, and let it flow
    Under his tail and over his crest;
      And through every feather   5
     Leaked the wet weather;
And the bough swung under his nest;
For his beak it was heavy with marrow.
    Is that the wind dying? O no;
    It's only two devils, that blow   10
     Through a murderer's bones, to and fro,
      In the ghosts' moonshine.

Ho! Eve, my grey carrion wife,
    When we have supped on kings' marrow,
Where shall we drink and make merry our life?   15
    Our nest it is queen Cleopatra's scull,
        'Tis cloven and cracked,
        And battered and hacked,
    But with tears of blue eyes it is full:
Let us drink then, my raven of Cairo.   20
    Is that the wind dying? O no;
    It's only two devils, that blow
    Through a murderer's bones, to and fro,
        In the ghosts' moonshine.

Dirge: We do lie beneath the grass

We do lie beneath the grass
    In the moonlight, in the shade
Of the yew-tree. They that pass
    Hear us not. We are afraid
        They would envy our delight,   5
        In our graves by glow-worm night.
Come follow us, and smile as we;
    We sail to the rock in the ancient waves,
Where the snow falls by thousands into the sea,
    And the drowned and the shipwrecked have happy graves.   10

Song from the Ship

To sea, to sea! the calm is o'er;
   The wanton water leaps in sport,
And rattles down the pebbly shore;
   The dolphin wheels, the sea-cows snort.
And unseen Mermaids' pearly song   5
Comes bubbling up, the weeds among.
   Fling broad the sail, dip deep the oar:
   To sea, to sea! the calm is o'er.

To sea, to sea! our wide-winged bark
   Shall billowy cleave its sunny way,   10
And with its shadow, fleet and dark,
   Break the caved Tritons' azure ray,
Like mighty eagle soaring light
O'er antelopes on Alpine height.
   The anchor heaves, the ship swings free,   15
   The sails swell full. To sea, to sea!

Song

I

In lover's ear a wild voice cried:
   'Sleeper, awake and rise!'
A pale form stood by his bed-side,
   With heavy tears in her sad eyes.
'A beckoning hand, a moaning sound,   5
A new-dug grave in weedy ground
For her who sleeps in dreams of thee.
Awake! Let not the murder be!'

Unheard the faithful dream did pray,
And sadly sighed itself away.   10
   'Sleep on,' sung Sleep, 'to-morrow
   'Tis time to know thy sorrow.'
   'Sleep on,' sung Death, 'to-morrow
   From me thy sleep thou'lt borrow.'
   Sleep on, lover, sleep on,   15
    The tedious dream is gone;
      The bell tolls one.

II

Another hour, another dream:
   'Awake! awake!' it wailed,
'Arise, ere with the moon's last beam   20
   Her rosy life hath paled.
A hidden light, a muffled tread,
A daggered hand beside the bed
Of her who sleeps and dreams of thee.
Thou wak'st not: let the murder be.'   25
In vain the faithful dream did pray,
And sadly sighed itself away.
   'Sleep on,' sung Sleep, 'to-morrow
   'Tis time to know thy sorrow.'
   'Sleep on,' sung Death, 'to-morrow   30
   From me thy sleep thou'lt borrow.'
   Sleep on, lover, sleep on,
    The tedious dream is gone;
      Soon comes the sun.

III

Another hour, another dream: 35
   A red wound on a snowy breast,
A rude hand stifling the last scream,
   On rosy lips a death-kiss pressed.

Blood on the sheets, blood on the floor,
The murderer stealing through the door. 40
'Now,' said the voice, with comfort deep,
'She sleeps indeed, and thou may'st sleep.'
The scornful dream then turned away
To the first, weeping cloud of day.
　'Sleep on,' sung Sleep, 'to-morrow 45
　'Tis time to know thy sorrow.'
　'Sleep on,' sung Death, 'to-morrow
　From me thy sleep thou'lt borrow.'
Sleep on, lover, sleep on,
The tedious dream is gone; 50
　The murder 's done.

Song on the Water

I

As mad sexton's bell, tolling
　For earth's loveliest daughter
Night's dumbness breaks rolling
　　Ghostlily:
So our boat breaks the water 5
　　Witchingly.

II

As her look the dream troubles
　Of her tearful-eyed lover,
So our sails in the bubbles
　　Ghostlily 10
　Are mirrored, and hover
　　Moonily.

Song from the Waters

The swallow leaves her nest,
The soul my weary breast;
But therefore let the rain
  On my grave
Fall pure; for why complain?   5
Since both will come again
  O'er the wave.

The wind dead leaves and snow
Doth hurry to and fro,
And, once, a day shall break   10
  O'er the wave,
When a storm of ghosts shall shake
The dead, until they wake
  In the grave.

Dream-Pedlary

I

If there were dreams to sell,
  What would you buy?
Some cost a passing bell;
  Some a light sigh,
That shakes from Life's fresh crown   5
Only a roseleaf down.
If there were dreams to sell,
Merry and sad to tell,
And the crier rung the bell,
  What would you buy?   10

A cottage lone and still,
   With bowers nigh,
Shadowy, my woes to still,
   Until I die.
Such pearl from Life's fresh crown   15
Fain would I shake me down.
Were dreams to have at will,
This would best heal my ill,
   This would I buy.

III

But there were dreams to sell,   20
   Ill didst thou buy;
Life is a dream, they tell,
   Waking, to die.
Dreaming a dream to prize,
Is wishing ghosts to rise;   25
   And, if I had the spell
   To call the buried, well,
      Which one would I?

IV

If there are ghosts to raise,
   What shall I call,   30
Out of hell's murky haze,
   Heaven's blue hall?
Raise my loved longlost boy
To lead me to his joy.
   There are no ghosts to raise;   35
   Out of death lead no ways;
      Vain is the call.

V

Know'st thou not ghosts to sue?
   No love thou hast.
Else lie, as I will do,   40
   And breathe thy last.
So out of Life's fresh crown
Fall like a rose-leaf down.
   Thus are the ghosts to woo;
   Thus are all dreams made true,   45
      Ever to last!

Alpine Spirit's Song

I

O'er the snow, through the air, to the mountain,
   With the antelope, with the eagle, ho!
   With a bound, with a feathery row,
To the side of the icy fountain,
   Where the gentians blue-belled blow.   5
Where the storm-sprite, the raindrops counting,
   Cowers under the bright rainbow;
    Like a burst of midnight fire,
    Singing shoots my fleet desire,
    Winged with the wing of love,   10
    Earth below and stars above.

II

Let me rest on the snow, never pressed
   But by chamois light and by eagle fleet,
   And the hearts of the antelope beat

'Neath the light of the moony cresset,   15
    Where the wild cloud rests his feet,
And the scented airs caress it
    From the alpine orchis sweet:
        And about the Sandalp lone
        Voices airy breathe a tone,   20
        Charming with the sense of love,
        Earth below and stars above.

III

Through the night, like a dragon from Pilate
    Out of murky cave, let us cloudy sail
    Over lake, over bowery vale,   25
As a chime of bells at twilight
    In the downy evening gale,
Passes swimming tremulously light;
    Till we reach yon rocky pale
        Of the mountain crowning all,   30
        Slumber there by waterfall,
        Lonely like a spectre's love,
        Earth beneath, and stars above.

Silenus in Proteus

Oh those were happy days, heaped up with wine-skins,
And ivy-wreathed and thyrsus-swinging days,
Swimming like streamy-tressed wanton Bacchantes,
When I was with thee and sat kingly on thee,
My ass of asses. Then quite full of wine—   5
Morning, eve—and leaning on a fawn,
Still pretty steady, and on t'other side

Some vinous-lipped nymph of Ariadne,
Her bosom a soft cushion for my right:
Half dreaming and half waking, both in bliss,   10
I sat upon my ass and laughed at Jove
But thou art dead, my dapple, and I too
Shall ride thee soon about the Elysian meadow,
Almost a skeleton as well as thou.
And why, oh dearest, could'st not keep thy legs   15
That sacred pair, sacred to sacred me?
Was this thy gratitude for pats and fondlings,
To die like any other mortal ass?
Was it for this, oh son of Semele,
I taught thee then, a little tumbling one,   20
To suck the goatskin oftener than the goat?

Lines Written in Switzerland

What silence drear in England's oaky forest,
Erst merry with the redbreast's ballad song
Or rustic roundelay! No hoof-print on the sward,
Where sometime danced Spenser's equestrian verse
Its mazy measure! Now by pathless brook   5
Gazeth alone the broken-hearted stag,
And sees no tear fall in from pitiful eye
Like kindest Shakespeare's. We, who marked how fell
Young Adonais, sick of vain endeavour
Larklike to live on high in tower of song;   10
And looked still deeper thro' each other's eyes
At every flash of Shelley's dazzling spirit,
Quivering like dagger on the breast of night,
That seemed some hidden natural light reflected
Upon time's scythe, a moment and away: 15

Darkness unfathomable over it
We, who have seen Mount Rydal's snowy head
Bound round with courtly jingles; list so long
Like old Orion for the break of morn,
Like Homer blind for sound of youthful harp;   20
And, if a wandering music swells the gale,
'Tis some poor solitary heartstring burst.
Well, Britain; let the fiery Frenchman boast
That at the bidding of the charmer moves
Their nation's heart, as ocean 'neath the moon   25
Silvered and soothed. Be proud of Manchester,
Pestiferous Liverpool, Ocean-Avernus,
Where bullying blasphemy, like a slimy lie,
Creeps to the highest church's pinnacle,
And glistening infects the light of heaven.   30
O flattering likeness on a copper coin!
Sit still upon your slave-raised cotton ball,
With upright toasting fork and toothless cat:
The country clown still holds her for a lion.
The voice, the voice! when the affrighted herds   35
Dash heedless to the edge of craggy abysses,
And the amazed circle of scared eagles
Spire to the clouds, amid the gletscher clash
When avalanches fall, nation-alarums—
But clearer, though not loud, a voice is heard   40
Of proclamation or of warning stern.
    Yet, if I tread out of the Alpine shade,
And once more weave the web of thoughtful verse,
May no vainglorious motive break my silence;
If I have sate unheard so long, it was in hope   45
That mightier and better might assay
The potent spell to break, which has fair Truth
Banished so drear a while from mouths of song.
Though genius, bearing out of other worlds
New freights of thought from fresh-discovered mines,   50

Be but reciprocated love of Truth:
Witness kind Shakespeare, our recording angel,
Newton, whose thought rebuilt the universe,
And Galileo, broken-hearted seer,
Who, like a moon attracted naturally,   55
Kept circling round the central sun of Truth.
Not in the popular playhouse, or full throng
Of opera-gazers longing for deceit;
Not on the velvet day-bed, novel-strewn,
Or in the interval of pot-and pipe;   60
Not between sermon and the scandalous paper,
May verse like this e'er hope an eye to feed on't.
But if there be, who, having laid the loved
Where they may drop a tear in roses' cups,
With half their hearts inhabit other worlds;   65
If there be any—ah! were there but few—
Who watching the slow lighting up of stars,
Lonely at eve, like seamen sailing near
Some island city where their dearest dwell,
Cannot but guess in sweet imagining—   70
Alas! too sweet, doubtful, and melancholy—
Which light is glittering from their loved one's home:
Such may perchance, with favourable mind,
Follow my thought along its mountainous path.
    Now then to Caucasus, the cavernous.—   75
[*Unfinished*]

EMILY BRONTË

I am the only being whose doom

May 17, 1837

I am the only being whose doom
No tongue would ask, no eye would mourn;
I never caused a thought of gloom,
A smile of joy, since I was born.

In secret pleasure, secret tears,   5
This changeful life has slipped away,
As friendless after eighteen years,
As lone as on my natal day.

There have been times I cannot hide,
There have been times when this was drear,   10
When my sad soul forgot its pride
And longed for one to love me here.

But those were in the early glow
Of feelings since subdued by care;
And they have died so long ago,   15
I hardly now believe they were.

First melted off the hope of youth,
Then fancy's rainbow fast withdrew;
And then experience told me truth
In mortal bosoms never grew.   20

'Twas grief enough to think mankind
All hollow, servile, insincere;
But worse to trust to my own mind
And find the same corruption there.

Alone I sat

August, 1837

Alone I sat; the summer day
Had died in smiling light away;
I saw it die, I watched it fade
From misty hill and breezeless glade;

And thoughts in my soul were gushing,   5
And my heart bowed beneath their power;
And tears within my eyes were rushing
Because I could not speak the feeling,
The solemn joy around me stealing
In that divine, untroubled hour   10

I asked myself, 'O why has heaven
Denied the precious gift to me,
The glorious gift to many given
To speak their thoughts in poetry?

'Dreams have encircled me,' I said,   15
'From careless childhood's sunny time;
Visions by ardent fancy fed
Since life was in its morning prime.'

But now, when I had hoped to sing,
My fingers strike a tuneless string;   20
And still the burden of the strain
Is 'Strive no more; 'tis all in vain.'

113

Lines: Far away is the land of rest

October, 1837

Far away is the land of rest,
Thousand miles are stretched between,
Many a mountain's stormy crest,
Many a desert void of green.

Wasted, worn is the traveller;   5
Dark his heart and dim his eye;
Without hope or comforter,
Faultering, faint, and ready to die.

Often he looks to the ruthless sky,
Often he looks o'er his dreary road,   10
Often he wishes down to lie
And render up life's tiresome load.

But yet faint not, mournful man;
Leagues on leagues are left behind
Since your sunless course began;   15
Then go on to toil resigned.

If you still despair control,
Hush its whispers in your breast,
You shall reach the final goal,
You shall win the land of rest.   20

Sleep brings no joy to me

November, 1837

Sleep brings no joy to me,
Remembrance never dies;
My soul is given to misery
And lives in sighs.

Sleep brings no rest to me;   5
The shadows of the dead
My waking eyes may never see
Surround my bed.

Sleep brings no hope to me;
In soundest sleep they come,   10
And with their doleful imagery
Deepen the gloom.

Sleep brings no strength to me,
No power renewed to brave,
I only sail a wilder sea,   15
A darker wave.

Sleep brings no friend to me
To soothe and aid to bear;
They all gaze, oh, how scornfully,
And I despair.   20

Sleep brings no wish to knit
My harassed heart beneath;
My only wish is to forget
In sleep of death.

Strong I stand, though I have borne

Strong I stand, though I have borne
Anger, hate, and bitter scorn;
Strong I stand, and laugh to see
How mankind have fought with me.

Shade of mast'ry, I contemn   5
All the puny ways of men;
Free my heart, my spirit free;
Beckon, and I'll follow thee.

False and foolish mortal, know,
If you scorn the world's disdain,   10
Your mean soul is far below
Other worms, however vain.

Thing of Dust—with boundless pride,
Dare you take me for a guide?
With the humble I will be;   15
Haughty men are naught to me.

To a Wreath of Snow

December —, 1837

O transient voyager of heaven!
O silent sign of winter skies!
What adverse wind thy sail has driven
To dungeons where a prisoner lies?

Methinks the hands that shut the sun   5
So sternly from this mourning brow
Might still their rebel task have done
And checked a thing so frail as thou.

116

They would have done it had they known
The talisman that dwelt in thee,   10
For all the suns that ever shone
Have never been so kind to me.

For many a week, and many a day,
My heart was weighed with sinking gloom,
When morning rose in mourning grey   15
And faintly lit my prison room;

But, angel like, when I awoke,
Thy silvery form so soft and fair,
Shining through darkness, sweetly spoke
Of cloudy skies and mountains bare—   20

The dearest to a mountaineer,
Who, all life long has loved the snow
That crowned her native summits drear
Better than greenest plains below.

And, voiceless, soulless messenger,   25
Thy presence waked a thrilling tone
That comforts me while thou art here
And will sustain when thou are gone.

Still as she looked the iron clouds

Still as she looked the iron clouds
Would part, and sunlight shone between,
But drearily strange and pale and cold.

117

Lines: *The soft unclouded blue of air*

April 28, 1839

The soft unclouded blue of air,
The earth as golden-green and fair
And bright as Eden's used to be:
That air and earth have rested me.

Laid on the grass I lapsed away,   5
Sank back again to childhood's day;
All harsh thoughts perished, memory mild
Subdued both grief and passion wild.

But did the sunshine even now
That bathed his stern and swarthy brow,   10
Oh, did it wake—I long to know—
One whisper, one sweet dream in him,
One lingering joy that years ago
Had faded—lost in distance dim?

That iron man was born like me,   15
And he was once an ardent boy:
He must have felt, in infancy,
The glory of a summer sky.

Though storms untold his mind have tossed,
He cannot utterly have lost   20
Remembrance of his early home—
So lost that not a gleam may come;

No vision of his mother's face
When she so fondly would set free
Her darling child from her embrace   25
To roam till eve at liberty:

Nor of his haunts, nor of the flowers
His tiny hand would grateful bear
Returning from the darkening bowers,
To weave into her glossy hair.   30

I saw the light breeze kiss his cheek,
His fingers 'mid the roses twined;
I watched to mark one transient streak
Of pensive softness shade his mind.

The open window showed around   35
A glowing park and glorious sky,
And thick woods swelling with the sound
Of Nature's mingled harmony.

Silent he sat. That stormy breast
At length, I said, has deigned to rest;   40
At length above that spirit flows
The waveless ocean of respose.

Let me draw near: 'twill soothe to view
His dark eyes dimmed with holy dew;
Remorse even now may wake within,   45
And half unchain his soul from sin.

Perhaps this is the destined hour
When hell shall lose its fatal power
And heaven itself shall bend above
To hail the soul redeemed by love.   50

Unmarked I gazed; my idle thought
Passed with the ray whose shine it caught;
One glance revealed how little care
He felt for all the beauty there.

Oh, crime can make the heart grow old   55
Sooner than years of wearing woe;
Can turn the warmest bosom cold
As winter wind or polar snow.

And now the house-dog stretched once more

July 12, 1839

And now the house-dog stretched once more
His limbs upon the glowing floor;
The children half resumed their play,
Though from the warm hearth scared away.
The goodwife left her spinning-wheel,   5
And spread with smiles the evening meal;
The shepherd placed a seat and pressed
To their poor fare his unknown guest.
And he unclasped his mantle now,
And raised the covering from his brow;   10
Said, 'Voyagers by land and sea
Were seldom feasted daintily';
And checked his host by adding stern
He'd no refinement to unlearn.
A silence settled on the room;   15
The cheerful welcome sank to gloom;
But not those words, though cold and high,
So froze their hospitable joy.
No—there was something in his face,
Some nameless thing they could not trace,   20
And something in his voice's tone
Which turned their blood as chill as stone.
The ringlets of his long black hair
Fell o'er a cheek most ghastly fair.

Youthful he seemed—but worn as they 25
Who spend too soon their youthful day.
When his glance drooped, 'twas hard to quell
Unbidden feelings' sudden swell;
And pity scarce her tears could hide,
So sweet that brow, with all its pride; 30
But when upraised his eye would dart
An icy shudder through the heart.
Compassion changed to horror then
And fear to meet that gaze again.
It was not hatred's tiger-glare, 35
Nor the wild anguish of despair;
It was not useless misery
Which mocks at friendship's sympathy.
No—lightning all unearthly shone
Deep in that dark eye's circling zone, 40
Such withering lightning as we deem
None but a spectre's look may beam;
And glad they were when he turned away
And wrapt him in his mantle grey,
Leant down his head upon his arm 45
And veiled from view his basilisk charm.

Sleep not, dream not

Sleep not, dream not; this bright day
Will not, cannot last for aye;
Bliss like thine is bought by years
Dark with torment and with tears.

Sweeter far than placid pleasure, 5
Purer, higher, beyond measure,
Yet alas the sooner turning
Into hopeless, endless mourning.

I love thee, boy; for all divine,
All full of God thy features shine.   10
Darling enthusiast, holy child,
Too good for this world's warring wild,
Too heavenly now but doomed to be
Hell-like in heart and misery.

And what shall change that angel brow   15
And quench that spirit's glorious glow?
Relentless laws that disallow
True virtue and true joy below.

And blame me not, if, when the dread
Of suffering clouds thy youthful head,   20
If when by crime and sorrow tost
Thy wandering bark is wrecked and lost.

I too depart, I too decline,
And make thy path no longer mine.
'Tis thus that human minds will turn,   25
All doomed alike to sin and mourn
Yet all with long gaze fixed afar,
Adoring virtue's distant star.

Mild the mist upon the hill

July 27, 1839

Mild the mist upon the hill,
Telling not of storms to-morrow;
No; the day has wept its fill,
Spent its store of silent sorrow.

Oh, I'm gone back to the days of youth,   5
I am a child once more;
And 'neath my father's sheltering roof,
And near the old hall door,

I watch this cloudy evening fall,
After a day of rain: 10
Blue mists, sweet mists of summer pall
The horizon's mountain-chain.

The damp stands in the long, green grass
As thick as morning's tears;
And dreamy scents of fragrance pass   15
That breathe of other years.

There was a time when my cheek burned

October, 1839

There was a time when my cheek burned
To give such scornful fiends the lie;
Ungoverned nature madly spurned
The law that bade it not defy.
O in the days of ardent youth   5
I would have given my life for truth.

For truth, for right, for liberty,
I would have gladly, freely died;
And now I calmly hear and see
The vain man smile, the fool deride;   10
Though not because my heart is tame,
Though not for fear, though not for shame.

My soul still chafes at every tone
Of selfish and self-blinded error;
My breast still braves the world alone,   15
Steeled as it ever was to terror;
Only I know, however I frown,
The same world will go rolling on.

The wind, I hear it sighing

October 29, 1839

The wind, I hear it sighing
With Autumn's saddest sound;
Withered leaves as thick are lying
As spring-flowers on the ground.

This dark night has won me   5
To wander far away;
Old feelings gather fast upon me
Like vultures round their prey.

Kind were they once, and cherished,
But cold and cheerless now;   10
I would their lingering shades had perished
When their light left my brow.

'Tis like old age pretending
The softness of a child,
My altered, hardened spirit bending   15
To meet their fancies wild.

Yet could I with past pleasures
Past woe's oblivion buy,
That by the death of my dearest treasures
My deadliest pains might die,   20

O then another daybreak
Might haply dawn above,
Another summer gild my cheek,
My soul, another love.

'Well, some may hate, and some may scorn'

November 14, 1839

'Well, some may hate, and some may scorn,
And some may quite forget thy name,
But my sad heart must ever mourn
Thy ruined hopes, thy blighted fame.'

'Twas thus I thought, an hour ago,   5
Even weeping o'er that wretch's woe.
One word turned back my gushing tears,
And lit my altered eye with sneers.

'Then bless the friendly dust,' I said,
'That hides thy unlamented head.   10
Vain as thou wert, and weak as vain,
The slave of falsehood, pride and pain,
My heart has nought akin to thine—
Thy soul is powerless over mine.'

But these were thoughts that vanished too—   15
Unwise, unholy, and untrue—
Do I despise the timid deer
Because his limbs are fleet with fear?

Or would I mock the wolf's death-howl
Because his form is gaunt and foul?   20
Or hear with joy the leveret's cry
Because it cannot bravely die?

No! Then above his memory
Let pity's heart as tender be:
Say, 'Earth lie lightly on that breast,   25
And, kind Heaven, grant that spirit rest!'

Start not! upon the minster wall

Start not! upon the minster wall,
Sunshine is shed in holy calm;
And, lonely though my footsteps fall,
The saints shall shelter thee from harm.

Shrink not if it be summer noon;   5
This shadow should night's welcome be.
These stairs are steep, but landed soon
We'll rest us long and quietly.

What though our path be o'er the dead?
They slumber soundly in the tomb;   10
And why should mortals fear to tread
The pathway to their future home?

And like myself lone, wholly lone

Feb. 27, 1841

And like myself lone, wholly lone,
It sees the day's long sunshine glow;
And like myself it makes its moan
In unexhausted woe.

Give we the hills our equal prayer: 5
Earth's breezy hills and heaven's blue sea;
We ask for nothing further here
But our own hearts and liberty.

Ah! could my hand unlock its chain,
How gladly would I watch it soar, 10
And ne'er regret and ne'er complain
To see its shining eyes no more.

But let me think that if to-day
It pines in cold captivity,
To-morrow both shall soar away, 15
Eternally, entirely Free.

I see around me tombstones grey

July 17, 1841

I see around me tombstones grey
Stretching their shadows far away.
Beneath the turf my footsteps tread
Lie low and lone the silent dead;
Beneath the turf, beneath the mould— 5
Forever dark, forever cold,
And my eyes cannot hold the tears
That memory hoards from vanished years;
For Time and Death and Mortal pain
Give wounds that will not heal again. 10
Let me remember half the woe
I've seen and heard and felt below,
And Heaven itself, so pure and blest,
Could never give my spirit rest.
Sweet land of light! thy children fair 15
Know nought akin to our despair;
Nor have they felt, nor can they tell
What tenants haunt each mortal cell,
What gloomy guests we hold within—
Torments and madness, tears and sin! 20

127

Well, may they live in extasy
Their long eternity of joy;
At least we would not bring them down
With us to weep, with us to groan.
No—Earth would wish no other sphere   25
To taste her cup of sufferings drear;
She turns from Heaven a careless eye
And only mourns that *we* must die!
Ah mother, what shall comfort thee
In all this boundless misery?   30
To cheer our eager eyes a while
We see thee smile; how fondly smile!
But who reads not through that tender glow
Thy deep, unutterable woe?
Indeed, no dazzling land above   35
Can cheat thee of thy children's love.
We all, in life's departing shine,
Our last dear longings blend with thine;
And struggle still and strive to trace
With clouded gaze, thy darling face.   40
We would not leave our native home
For *any* world beyond the Tomb.
No—rather on thy kindly breast
Let us be laid in lasting rest;
Or waken but to share with thee   45
A mutual immortality.

O *thy bright eyes must answer now*

O thy bright eyes must answer now,
When Reason, with a scornful brow,
Is mocking at my overthrow;
O thy sweet tongue must plead for me
And tell why I have chosen thee!   5

Stern Reason is to judgement come
Arrayed in all her forms of gloom:
Wilt thou my advocate be dumb?
No, radiant angel, speak and say
Why I did cast the world away;   10

Why I have persevered to shun
The common paths that others run;
And on a strange road journeyed on
Heedless alike of Wealth and Power—
Of Glory's wreath and Pleasure's flower.   15

These once indeed seemed Beings divine,
And they perchance heard vows of mine
And saw my offerings on their shrine—
But, careless gifts are seldom prized,
And mine were worthily despised;   20

So with a ready heart I swore
To seek their altar-stone no more,
And gave my spirit to adore
Thee, ever present, phantom thing—
My slave, my comrade, and my King!   25

A slave because I rule thee still;
Incline thee to my changeful will
And make thy influence good or ill—
A comrade, for by day and night
Thou art my intimate delight—   30

My Darling Pain that wounds and seers
And wrings a blessing out from tears
By deadening me to real cares;
And yet, a king—though prudence well
Have taught thy subject to rebel.   35

And am I wrong to worship where
Faith cannot doubt nor Hope despair
Since my own soul can grant my prayer?
Speak, God of Visions, plead for me
And tell why I have chosen thee!   40

October 14, 1844

Remembrance

March 3, 1845

Cold in the earth, and the deep snow piled above thee!
Far, far removed, cold in the dreary grave!
Have I forgot, my Only Love, to love thee,
Severed at last by Time's all-wearing wave?

Now, when alone, do my thoughts no longer hover   5
Over the mountains on that northern shore;
Resting their wings where heath and fern-leaves cover
That noble heart for ever, ever more?

Cold in the earth, and fifteen wild Decembers
From those brown hills have melted into spring—   10
Faithful indeed is the spirit that remembers
After such years of change and suffering!

Sweet Love of youth, forgive if I forget thee
While the World's tide is bearing me along:
Sterner desires and darker hopes beset me,   15
Hopes which obscure but cannot do thee wrong.

No other Sun has lightened up my heaven;
No other Star has ever shone for me:
All my life's bliss from thy dear life was given—
All my life's bliss is in the grave with thee.   20

But when the days of golden dreams had perished
And even Despair was powerless to destroy,
Then did I learn how existence could be cherished,
Strengthened and fed without the aid of joy;

Then did I check the tears of useless passion,   25
Weaned my young soul from yearning after thine;
Sternly denied its burning wish to hasten
Down to that tomb already more than mine!

And even yet, I dare not let it languish,
Dare not indulge in Memory's rapturous pain;   30
Once drinking deep of that divinest anguish,
How could I seek the empty world again?

Death, that struck when I was most confiding

April 10, 1845

Death, that struck when I was most confiding
In my certain Faith of Joy to be,
Strike again, Time's withered branch dividing
From the fresh root of Eternity!

Leaves, upon Time's branch, were growing brightly,   5
Full of sap and full of silver dew;
Birds, beneath its shelter, gathered nightly;
Daily, round its flowers, the wild bees flew.

Sorrow passed and plucked the golden blossom,
Guilt stripped off the foliage in its pride;   10
But, within its parent's kindly bosom,
Flowed forever Life's restoring tide.

Little mourned I for the parted Gladness,
For the vacant nest and silent song;
Hope was there and laughed me out of sadness,   15
Whispering, 'Winter will not linger long.'

And behold, with tenfold increase blessing
Spring adorned the beauty-burdened spray;
Wind and rain and fervent heat caressing
Lavished glory on its second May.   20

High it rose; no winged grief could sweep it;
Sin was scared to distance with its shine:
Love and its own life had power to keep it
From all wrong, from every blight but thine!

Heartless Death, the young leaves droop and languish!   25
Evening's gentle air may still restore—
No: the morning sunshine mocks my anguish—
Time for me must never blossom more!

Strike it down, that other boughs may flourish
Where that perished sapling used to be;   30
Thus, at least, its mouldering corpse will nourish
That from which it sprung—Eternity.

No coward soul is mine

Jan. 2, 1846

No coward soul is mine
No trembler in the world's storm-troubled sphere
I see Heaven's glories shine
And Faith shines equal arming me from Fear

O God within my breast   5
Almighty ever-present Deity
Life, that in me hast rest
As I Undying Life, have power in Thee

Vain are the thousand creeds
That move men's hearts, unutterably vain,   10
Worthless as withered weeds
Or idlest froth amid the boundless main

To waken doubt in one
Holding so fast by thy infinity
So surely anchored on   15
The steadfast rock of Immortality

With wide-embracing love
Thy spirit animates eternal years
Pervades and broods above,
Changes, sustains, dissolves, creates and rears   20

Though Earth and moon were gone
And suns and universes ceased to be
And thou wert left alone
Every Existence would exist in thee

There is not room for Death   25
Nor atom that his might could render void
Since thou art Being and Breath
And what thou art may never be destroyed.

COMMENTARY AND NOTES

GEORGE DARLEY

LIFE

George Darley was born in Ireland in 1795. He was the son of gifted parents, who, however, went to America while he was still an infant, leaving him and two of his sisters in charge of a grandfather. When they returned, they found that George had developed a severe hesitation in his speech. This stammer, reminiscent of Lamb's, was to grow worse with the years, leading Darley to withdraw ever further from social contact.

Nevertheless, he was a successful student, giving evidence of the intellectual distinction which appears in his later critical writings. In 1820 he took his B.A. at Trinity College, Dublin, and he may well have hoped for a fellowship: but he was not offered one, and he set off for London, where he became a freelance writer. He established himself quickly as one of the brightest talents of the day, and became notorious, under the pseudonym of John Lacy, as the incisively severe drama critic of the *London Magazine*, to which he became a contributor in 1823. After travelling on the Continent during 1830 he developed an interest in painting, and on his return he began to write as an art critic for the *Athenaeum*. He also published several textbooks on mathematics. It is possible that this mathematical work relaxed his mind, but we know from a long letter of his to Miss Mitford that he hated the drudgery and bitterness of reviewing, which he regarded as a distraction from his poetic vocation.

Although he published a good deal of creative work, Darley never achieved great renown. His first slim volume was *The Errors of Ecstasie*, which appeared in 1822. In 1826 a collection of prose tales and sketches was published with the title *Labours of Idleness*. Darley's pastoral play *Sylvia*, his most ambitious work so far, came out in 1827, and its failure greatly disheartened him. It was at this time that he temporarily abandoned literature for mathematics. 1835 saw the circulation of a private edition of *Nepenthe*, of which more will be said shortly. In the eleven years which now remained to him Darley published little verse—a few lyrics in magazines, but no further collection. He turned instead to the drama, as did many of his contemporaries. Darley was critically well prepared, both through his journalistic work and through his work in editing Beaumont and Fletcher (his edition was published in 1840). *Thomas à Becket* (1840), his first historical drama, showed much promise, and Henry Crabbe Robinson refers to it as 'a work of genius'. It made only a moderate public impression, however, and its successor *Ethelstan* (1841) was an outright failure. This play was its author's last creative work of any significance.

POETRY

Darley was a minor poet and, by his own standards, must be considered a failure. But this was in an age when to be minor and a failure was to some extent creditable. Writing after the full tide of Romanticism, from Words-worth to Shelley, had subsided, and the influence of Byron, which Darley deplored, was paramount, he had strong and clearly formulated views on what poetry should be; but his personal qualities were not such as to enable him to impose these views on his time, or even, in any marked degree, imprint them on his own work. He lacked drive, assurance, perhaps even ambition. It was left to such poets as Tennyson and Mrs Browning to represent the ideals of early Victorian readers. Darley was only too painfully aware of his personal limitations. Indeed, he almost made a virtue of them. In an article entitled *The Enchanted Lyre* he wrote:

> I was, in fine, such an incomprehensible, unsystematised, impersonal compound of opposite qualities, with no overwhelming power of mind to carry off, as I have seen in others, these heterogeneous particles in a flood of intellectuality, that I quickly perceived obscurity was the sphere in which nature had destined me to shine, and that the very best compliment my friends could pay me, when I had left them, was to forget me and my thoughts for ever.

Darley believed that contemporary poetry had degenerated into the sentimentality and pretty-prettiness of popular poets such as Barry Cornwall on the one hand and the rhetorical hollowness of Byron and his imitators on the other. He expressed strong disapproval of Byron's influence on the poetic drama of the time; but in attempting this form, he himself followed a will o' the wisp that had misled others and was to mislead more. Poetic drama was dead long before the beginning of Victoria's reign, but the poets were very slow to acknowledge this. In any case, Darley's own views and inclinations were not in the direction of drama but of lyric. He believed that poetry should approximate to song, and that rhythm was the poet's central inspiration. He had a good ear which, however, sometimes failed him. Yet the sound of his poems is often fresh and refreshing when we are jaded by the almost mechanical impeccability of Tennyson. He sought a way out of the impasse at which poetry had arrived by going backwards—to the Middle Ages, to the Elizabethans and the seventeenth century. There are in his lyrics many echoes of Shakespeare. The diction which Darley accordingly adopted was artificial in the extreme. There is a time for artificiality, as distinct from naturalness, in the diction of poetry: although Darley's style never fully emerges from artificiality long enough to make a powerful impact, it is difficult to see what other course a man of his beliefs and his temperament could have taken. It is true, but almost superfluous, to say, as Ian Jack says: 'Few poets have in their language so little contact with the spoken idiom of their own day.' Darley, the congenital stammerer, would probably have been the first to admit this, though he would not have regarded it as a fault. 'In Darley,' writes Heath-Stubbs, his most perceptive critic, 'we seem to discern an independent mind, running in many things counter to the tendencies of his age but without sufficient strength and confidence in himself to establish his position as a rebel.' He was, Heath-Stubbs claims, a 'highly original writer and in the direct line of succession from Keats and Shelley, and also from Blake'.

Darley's pastoral play *Sylvia* was a failure, and is chiefly remarkable for its lyrics. The best of his work, however, is to be found in *Nepenthe*, where his real command of striking and imaginative imagery, and richness and sonority of language find their best expression. His debt to Shelley and Keats, and especially to such symbolic dream-poems as *Alastor* and *Endymion*, is obvious. His best lyric, however, *O blest unfabled incense tree*, is immediately reminiscent of Coleridge. It deserves to be better known, and is one of the few nineteenth-century poems worthy to be judged alongside *Kubla Khan*. In other lyrics, such as *The Demon's Cave*, there is evidence of a macabre, Jacobean sensibility. *O May, thou art a merry time* is an effective exercise in Elizabethan lyric. In *Siren Chorus* the clear-cut imagery and imaginative range are notable, but lyrics such as *Final Chorus* will offend some readers by the artificiality of their over-poetic diction. *A Sea Dream* is an attractive evocation of a submarine landscape, and it is such poems as this which incline us to say that the further Darley is from mundane realities, the happier he is. It is, moreover, almost a truism to say that Darley's inspiration, as he himself knew, was almost wholly literary. In the end, this must count against him. But perhaps it is better to be a good, original and interesting literary poet than one of no technical accomplishment concerned with day-to-day realities. *It is not beauty I demand* is a successful and committed pastiche of seventeenth-century lyric—so successful that it was, as every editor points out, included by Palgrave in the first editions of his *Golden Treasury* as an anonymous Cavalier song.

NOTES ON THE POEMS OF GEORGE DARLEY

p. 1   from *Nepenthe*
Three separate sections form the very long poem.

1–57 A lyrical celebration, evocative of Shakespeare (see *The Phoenix and the Turtle*), Keats and Coleridge, of the fabulous bird variously referred to in classical and medieval literature. Variations on the myth are numerous, but the general sense is that of a very beautiful bird sacred to the sun and living somewhere in the Levant; only one of its kind exists at a time, and after a very long life it is renewed by setting fire to itself in a fragrant tree, being miraculously reborn from its own ashes.
98 *Nepenthe:* 'A drug of Egyptian origin mentioned in the Odyssey as capable of banishing grief or trouble from the mind' (*OED*).
99 *what boots:* what is the use.

p. 4   *The Demon's Cave*

2 *Fen-pamper'd:* i.e. fed or enriched by moisture from the fens.
6 *Cyclops' mountain-home:* the cave of the legendary one-eyed giants in Sicily (*Odyssey*).

p. 5   *O May, thou art a merry time*

7 *tabor:* a small side-drum used in conjunction with a pipe in Elizabethan days to accompany country dancing: note that this song, reminiscent of Shakespeare (see *A Winter's Tale*, etc.), is strongly Elizabethan in flavour.

p. 6 Noon in the Forest

70 *cushat:* wood pigeon.

p. 10 Final Chorus

1–3 See Shakespeare, *Merchant of Venice* IV.1.1 184 ff.

p. 11 To be or not to be
This Shakespearean pastiche has power, because the theme was one very close to Darley's thinking. It is not unworthy to be compared with the original soliloquy in *Hamlet* (III,1,56 ff.).

7 *velleity:* wishful state, feeble desires.
15 *fleering:* jeering, mocking.
30 *un–Atlantic:* not like the shoulders of the giant Atlas, who, in classical mythology, was condemned to bear the weight of the whole world.
32 *fluxion:* movement.

p. 14 To my Tyrant
The imagery of this love lyric is drawn from the Wars of the Roses between the rival houses of York and Lancaster.

p. 14 It is not Beauty I demand
While Darley's skill in imitating the Cavalier lyrists no doubt justified a Victorian editor in including this in the first edition of Palgrave's *Golden Treasury* as an anonymous sixteenth-century song, a modern editor, more familiar with the seventeenth century, would probably be suspicious of certain lines, such as 19–20 and 26.

10 *Hebe:* daughter of Zeus and Hera, associated with eternal youth.
20 *Ilium:* Troy.
27 *Siren:* One of the women in Greek mythology whose beautiful voices lured sailors to their doom.

HARTLEY COLERIDGE

Hartley Coleridge, the eldest son of Samuel Taylor Coleridge, was born prematurely on 19 September 1796. Three months later the family moved from Somerset to the Lake District, where Hartley was to pass most of his boyhood. The next few years were for Coleridge the happiest and most productive of his adult life, and it was during this time that he wrote *Frost at Midnight*, in which can be seen the intense and tender mixture of love and hope that he lavished on his son. Hartley was to be the fulfilment of the Wordsworthian philosophy of childhood. He was the 'six years' darling of a pygmy size' of the *Intimations Ode*, and for the moment he was 'a spirit dancing on an aspen leaf—unwearied in joy—from morning to night, indefatigably joyous'.

'It is a cruel thing to breed up boys alone', Hartley was later to write; and while his mind developed rapidly under the influence of nature and the brilliant conversation of his father, of William and Dorothy Wordsworth and their many distinguished visitors, he lacked the abrasive contact of children with less imagination. For the rest of his life he was to be dogged by an inability to form easy and permanent relationships. He was, however, a delightful child; Coleridge wrote, 'Hartley is considered a genius by Wordsworth and Southey, indeed by everyone who has seen much of him'. He was allowed to live in his imagination unchecked, and if he often astounded his father's friends, he also worried them. They could see how he was rapidly becoming a dreamer divorced from reality, whose fantasies were undermining his will-power. His intellectual precocity disturbed them too. The boy himself saw the root of the trouble when he said to his father: 'The pity is that I was always thinking of my thoughts'.

From school, where he rarely took part in games but entertained his companions with long and complicated stories, he gained a Post-Mastership at Merton College, Oxford. It was here that he first began to write poetry seriously. Intelligent but shy, he would set great hopes on winning the annual verse prize as something that would give him the attention he so craved, particularly from women, who he was convinced had an aversion to him, partly because of his small stature. He failed in his hopes and began to drink. Alcoholism remained with him intermittently for the rest of his life. Having been unsuccessful in the rigorous probationary year for his fellowship at Oriel, his outbursts of spontaneous excitement and his willingness to talk to everybody being regarded as improper, he tried, again unsuccessfully, to support himself by writing in London. His failure to gain the Oriel fellowship was to be a constant burden on his conscience. Shortly before his own death Coleridge wrote with great insight and sympathy:

Poor dear Hartley! He was hardly—nay, cruelly—used by the Oriel men—and it fell with a more crushing weight upon him, that with all his defects Love had followed him like his shadow and still does. If you can conceive, in connection with an excellent heart, sound religious principles, a mind constitutionally religious, and lastly an active and powerful intellect —if you can conceive, I say, in connection with all these, not a mania, not a derangement, but an idiocy of Will or rather of Volition, you will have formed a tolerably correct conception of Hartley Coleridge.

Hartley returned to the Lake District to teach and write and be near his father's friends. The school he ran at Ambleside failed. The image of his father was always in front of him, and although he would criticize his writings with great insight, he could never see his defects as a man. He felt hopelessly inferior before the greater muscularity of Coleridge's mind, and he often wondered if he was accepted only for his sake. The one volume of poems that he published in his lifetime, in 1833, was dedicated to him. 'Li'le Hartley', as they called him, was greatly loved by the cottagers of the Lakes, far more indeed than the lofty Wordsworth. A convinced Christian, he had a genuine and uncondescending tenderness when in company, but alone in his study he examined his tortured conscience, his failure to live up to his early promise and what he thought was his own unsuitability for love. The victim, perhaps, of a too intensely lived childhood, he died in 1849.

POETRY

Hartley Coleridge's fame, such as it is, rests chiefly on his sonnets. He has been called 'after Shakespeare our *sweetest* English sonneteer', and the judgement is probably well founded. The Petrarcan form came most naturally to him, since its more massive quality allows for less counter-pointed patterns of thought than the Shakespearean, whose wit and poise were something alien to his prevailing mood and to the spirit of Romantic poetry. Besides, a sonnet was something he could write at a single sitting, and he always wrote in direct response to a poetic 'fit'. Friends reported that they had seen him write the first draft of a sonnet in ten minutes. When the mood was over, he might put at the bottom of a page such a comment as 'Worth hammering at'. Like Wordsworth, by whom he was as deeply influenced as by his father, he composed aloud, and ideas often came to him when out walking. The villagers, who held him in great affection, supplied him with paper and pencils as he knocked at their doors, a nearly completed poem in his head. The quality of his best work is thus a spontaneity that came partly from his complete mastery of the form he adopted. He himself best describes his methods of composition:

> . . . I cannot foresee. Of all my verses, not a single copy was begun with any definite purpose. In every sonnet the idea has come upon me in the course of composition—sometimes it may be suggested by a rhyme—and yet if my own judgement be trustworthy, they are not deficient in singleness or completeness.

However, the sonnet was not the only form in which Hartley excelled. He had a sensitive ear and wrote lyrics of unique poignancy, while his short and most intense poems are unduly neglected. He was competent too at blank verse, but was unable to sustain a strong mood. His one completed narrative poem, an appallingly melodramatic piece entitled *Leonard and Susan*, contains this admirable passage:

> 'Tis sweet to see
> The day dawn creeping gradual o'er the sky:
> The silent sun at noon is bright and fair,
> And the calm eve is lovely; but 'tis sad
> To sink at eve on the dark dewy turf,
> And feel that none in all the countless host
> Of glimmering stars beholds one little spot,
> One humble home of thine.

The feeling of isolation that this conveys, an isolation stronger than the somewhat wistful consolation of nature, is typical of Hartley. In other poems we see how deep it went; for, like his father, he was haunted by the phantom of 'Life in death' and knew too well that grief without a pang, void, dark and drear' with which Coleridge described the Romantic wasteland. Yet Hartley lacked the energy and heroism that gave his father that primary vision of sterile hopelessness. He was forced to think round the subject and convey it in a minor mode. Early winter is the season of death in life, and for Hartley November had a particular significance. The month is an obvious enough parallel to his own prevailing feelings, but how delicately he treats it in his best-known sonnet, entitled *November*. The cadences are beautifully modulated, and the observation is exquisite. It is the mark of maturity in a minor poet that he can say the obvious with a delicate and unforced originality.

From seeing November in his soul it was natural that Hartley should pass to meditation on death. His outlook is coloured by Christian stoicism, and for this reason he avoids the sensational and the macabre on the one hand and the profoundly melancholy on the other. The quality of his faith was not that which necessarily leads to the most moving expression, since it consists of a too simple rejection of the world and a too easy belief in the consolation of Heaven, so that often we get neither a sense of the greatness of man's struggle in the world nor of the transfiguring clarity of paradise. Heaven, indeed, is too simply a meeting-place for old friends. Hartley was able to transcend this simplistic approach, however, and distil the essence of great drama, as his poem *Death-bed Reflections of Michelangelo* reveals.

'Pray in darkness if there be no light'—such was Hartley's religion, but it was only a part of his personality, and it should only be seen in terms of the rest. If his sonnets on biblical subjects are rather grim, it should be remembered that he found a real joy in the innocence of children, and was loved by everyone who met him for his spontaneous kindness. What helped to save him from total despair, too, was his sense of humour, which enabled him to write a few pieces of excellent satire, including his felicitous parody of Wordsworth.

Hartley translated at least two of Petrarch's sonnets, and one element in his own love poetry is a similarly intense idealization of purity, which raises the beloved to an unattainable region towards which the lover's soul aspires. For Hartley this was both a convention and a psychological need. The exaltation of the beloved in this way simplifies and beautifies passion until it becomes the highest expression of love's sanctity, as we can see in the sonnet beginning 'I loved thee once, when every thought of mine'. The danger of such love is that it becomes divorced from real human contact, while on the level of poetry a belief in the impossibility of love leads to self-pity, and this is something from which Hartley is not always free. What he did excel in, however—and his intense observation, his

143

unhappy childhood and his own bachelor state enhanced this—was the portrayal of simple domesticity. Although it clearly owes something to passages in *Frost at Midnight*, his sonnet beginning 'The crackling embers on the hearth are dead' is a good poem.

Hartley had a high, if not original, conception of what the poet should be. His ideal is a social one. The poet is one whose lines 'live in the souls of men like household words', and who knows that there is truth, freedom and virtue in positive inspiration. He thought that his own work hardly stood up to this test. 'No hope have I to live a deathless name', he wrote, and went on to analyse the reason: he lived at too great a distance from that which gives the power to 'bestow unfading life on transient bliss'. He wrote because he loved poetry and because it had given him consolation. Yet if he failed to be a major poet because, to use his father's distinction, he wrote with his fancy and not with his imagination, he is not for that reason to be dismissed. He has been too much neglected.

NOTES ON THE POEMS OF HARTLEY COLERIDGE

p. 19   *Youth, love, and mirth . . .*

2 *the Prodigal:* a reference to the parable of the prodigal son.

p. 20   *Night*
A poem which Hartley declared was 'partly inspired by the German of Ludwig Tiek'.

p. 20   *I thank my God . . .*
The first line of this sonnet is italicized since it is a quotation from the close of the preceding one in a series.

13 *Sabbath:* the last day of the week and a period of rest according to Jewish law.

p. 22   *What is young passion . . .*

vernal: spring-like.

p. 24 Regeneration

8 *Lethe:* one of the four rivers of Hell, its waters were said to grant forgetfulness.

21 *Magdalen:* one of the three Maries of the New Testament and a repentant prostitute.

25 *Bethesda:* a pool in Jerusalem. See John 5.2.

p. 26 To Somebody

The epigraph to this poem comes from *A Midsummer Night's Dream* Act 2 Sc. 1.

p. 28 Expertus Loquitur

The epigraph translates the Latin title of this work.

p. 30 Poietes Apoietes

The title may be translated as The Fame of the Poet

p. 32 Death-bed Reflections of Michelangelo

The poem recounts Michelangelo's skill not only as a sculptor, but as a painter, poet and architect too.

9 *a temple for mankind:* St Peter's in Rome.

p. 35 I have been cherish'd . . .

4 A reference to his father, Samuel Taylor Coleridge. The poem expresses well the situation of the son of a great man.

p. 36 When we are dead . . .

Hartley's own note reads: 'Wordsworth, being born at Cockermouth might be styled the Gander of Cocker, as Shakespeare was termed the Swan of Avon.'

1 *Davy's Locker:* a nautical term for death.

p. 37   He lived amidst th'untrodden ways . . .
This is a satire on Wordsworth in the form of a parody of one of the
'Lucy Poems' which begins 'She dwelt among the untrodden ways . . .'

2 *Rydal Lake:* the lake near Wordsworth's house, Rydal Mount.
9 *'Milk- white Doe':* a reference to Wordsworth's poem 'The White Doe
of Rylstone'.
11 *Longman's:* Wordsworth's publishers.

THOMAS HOOD

LIFE

Thomas Hood was born in London in 1799. Although his father was a
partner in a firm of booksellers and his mother the sister of Sands, the
engraver, his education does not appear to have been planned to fit him for
a literary or artistic career. He attended various private schools in London
until he was about thirteen, when he entered a merchant's counting-house.
It is possible that the death of his father, which occurred in 1811, made it
financially necessary for the young Hood to take a job; but he was of a
delicate constitution, and his health soon failed. He was sent to relatives in
Dundee to recover his strength, and he remained there until 1818, passing
his time in reading, writing for local newspapers and sketching. On his
return to London he became an apprentice engraver, working first for
his uncle and later for John le Keux. Again, however, his health proved to
be too weak to withstand the confinement which this trade imposed on him,
and it was at this time that he decided on a literary and journalistic career.
Taylor and Hessey, the publishers, had been friends of Hood's father, and
they offered him a job as an assistant sub-editor on their *London Magazine*.
He was a constant contributor for the next two years, and the verses of
which his contributions largely consisted anticipate his later work both
stylistically and in their content.

The year 1821, in which he began to work for Taylor and Hessey, was
crucial to Hood's development. It was at this time that he met the literary
circle which centred on Charles Lamb. He became acquainted, not only
with Lamb himself, but also with De Quincey, Hazlitt, Allan Cunningham

and John Hamilton Reynolds, all of whom were members of the brilliant staff of the *London Magazine*. With the last named in particular he established a close friendship, cemented by his marriage in 1824 to Reynolds' sister Jane. It was the death of their first child which Lamb wrote of in his lines *On an Infant dying as soon as born*. Reynolds and Hood collaborated in writing *Odes and Addresses to Great People*, published anonymously in 1825 and ascribed by Coleridge to Charles Lamb.

By now Hood was a full-time writer. His comic-grotesque manner became very popular, and his *Whims and Oddities*, published in 1826, were successful enough to be followed in 1827 by a second series under the same title. In 1829 he took over the editorship of the *Gem*, an annual which distinguished itself by publishing some of Tennyson's early work. Even more successful than the *Gem* was *The Comic Annual*, a more substantial publication which first appeared in 1830.

Hood's life in these years was crowded, and one cannot help feeling that he devoted himself all too wholeheartedly to the production of mediocre but profitable journalistic verse. Nevertheless, he did find time to write some serious poetry. In 1827 *The Plea of the Midsummer Fairies* appeared, revealing a Keatsian Hood who had not been in evidence in much of the journalistic work. Although Keats himself had died in 1821, it would seem that his admirer Reynolds encouraged Hood to read the poems of his dead friend, and thus brought the young poet under his influence. Commercially, however, the book was a complete failure: Hood was to restrict himself in future to the publication of more popular and marketable verse.

In 1834 he met with sudden financial disaster. The causes of this are not clear, but it is probable that the bankruptcy of a publisher was to blame. By declaring himself insolvent Hood might have escaped the worst results of his misfortune, but he chose to forfeit all his property to his creditors and to live on the advances which his publishers paid him. He left London with his family and went to live on the Continent, hoping that this would enable him to reduce his expenditure while he worked to clear himself of debt. There was a violent storm during the crossing to Holland in March 1835, and this further weakened the poet's sickly constitution. The Hoods settled first in Coblenz and later in Ostend, and Hood's Continental travels are the basis of his books *Hood's Own* (1838) and *Up the Rhine* (1839). *The Comic Annual* also continued to appear, and in 1840 the family was able to return to England and settle in Camberwell. Hood threw himself once more into London journalism, first contributing to, and later editing, *The New*

Monthly Magazine. In 1844 he began a new undertaking, to be called *Hood's Magazine*, but his health broke down, and his last months were spent in a state of acute exhaustion. He was confined to bed from Christmas 1844 until his death in May 1845.

This period was not entirely wretched, however. Sir Robert Peel granted him an annual pension of £100, which his widow was to continue to receive after his death. More important, perhaps, to Hood himself, *The Song of the Shirt*, published anonymously in the Christmas 1843 edition of *Punch*, achieved a popularity unprecedented even among his own works. Hood quite failed to emulate the high example of Keats, but he won the real affection of the citizens of London. A public monument was erected above his grave in Kensal Green Cemetery, adorned with bas-reliefs depicting scenes from *Eugene Aram's Dream* and *The Bridge of Sighs*, and bearing the inscription: 'He sang the Song of the Shirt'.

POETRY

Despite his hope that he would be read as a serious poet, Hood was accepted by his contemporaries chiefly as a comic versifier, humorist and punster. To relieve his chronically strained financial position he wrote a great deal of polite and facile album verse, becoming, indeed, something of a verse journalist. Nevertheless, he must be considered one of the chief poets in that sterile period between the deaths of Shelley and Keats and the rise of Tennyson and Browning. His later attempts to portray the pathos of city and working-class life, a rare feature in English Romantic verse, and something more successfully achieved in the novel, shows both his originality and his limitations.

Hood's only published volume of serious poetry appeared in 1827 and was a failure. It contains such poems as *The Plea of the Midsummer Fairies* and, more especially, the *Ode to Autumn*, which show how pervasive was the influence of Keats upon him. We find in these poems a studied mellifluousness of language and luxurious, dream-like imagery. Yet there is about them the mannered quality of all imitation, and they lack the precision and control, the awareness of pain rather than pathos that marks the mature work of Keats. Another theme that Hood took from Keats and expanded was a concern, already traceable in the work of Beddoes, amounting at times to an obsession, with death and decay. Wishing, no doubt, to give profundity to his work, Hood more often succeeded in portraying mere melodrama. There is a crudity of approach here, and it is not always relieved by his use of language. *The Last Man*, which was an extremely popular poem, is a good example of this.

The Last Man has obvious affinities with both *The Ancient Mariner* and with parts of the Old Testament. It attempts to depict an overwhelming isolation through the use of the macabre, but Coleridge's poem, partly through the terseness of the ballad form, always achieves the awesome and the mysterious and never descends to the merely sensational. Hood's poem is looser and less powerful.

> So I went and cut his body down
>   To bury it decentlie;
>   God send there were any good soul alive
>   To do the like by me!
>   But the wild dogs came with terrible speed
>   And bade me up the tree.

We find in the poem too that harsh, Hebraic outlook that Matthew Arnold was to note sadly in his contemporaries. The personality is forgotten at the expense of religious generalizations, and this, rather naturally, incurs a loss of humanity or even of generous humour, such humanity and humour as we find in *The Two Peacocks of Bedfont*. This poem does reveal, however, that Hood had a keen eye for detail, and throughout his life he was a great admirer of the art of Hogarth.

In *The Song of the Shirt*, written towards the end of his life, we find a new power in Hood's work. Feeling has replaced a too easy moralizing, and a genuine social concern emerges, despite the unintentional humour arising from the excessive use of repetition. Clearly it was popular, since it is one of the poems recorded on his monument. Perhaps Hood was at his best in short poems; while the imagery of *Silence* is striking and memorable, his sonnet *To an Enthusiast* closes with these fine and original lines:

> For as the current of thy life shall flow,
> Gilded by shine of sun or shadow-stain'd,
> Through flow'ry valley or unwholesome fen,
> Thrice blessed in thy joy or in thy woe
> Thrice cursed of thy race,—thou art ordain'd
> To share beyond the lot of common men.

Ian Jack writes that there is 'something almost pathological about Hood's pruning', and to a certain extent he is right, though there is no doubt that it was an easy and profitable mannerism. An interest in language is a primary, perhaps *the* primary, qualification for a poet, and this almost inevitably leads to a fascination with word-play. At its best, the pun forces the reader to concentrate on two simultaneous ideas, and thus keeps the expression fresh, compact and complex. At its worst, when it serves no significant function, it becomes a Christmas cracker jingle. This is something that Hood does not always avoid; indeed, it is usually deliberate, and this example shows how sterile the ballad tradition is becoming in Romantic poetry:

> The body-snatchers they have come,
> And made a snatch at me;
> It's very hard them kind of men
> Won't let a body be!

But it is unfair to leave Hood on this note. He was a sensitive man who led an unhappy life, coming to his maturity at a time of poetic dearth. It is inevitable too that his poems should not stand up well to a comparison with those of men of extraordinary genius such as the earlier generation of the Romantics.

NOTES ON THE POEMS OF THOMAS HOOD

p. 39 Ode: Autumn
The mood, movement and imagery of this poem is an obvious exercise in Keatsian imitation.

21 *Proserpine:* Proserpina (Latin) was the Greek Persephone, daughter of Demeter, and was carried off while gathering flowers to be the wife of Hades, King of the underworld.

p. 41 The Last Man
9 *duds:* clothes.
15 *orts:* scraps of food.
109 *mumping:* sulky, grumbling.

p. 49 from The Plea of the Midsummer Fairies
The first six descriptive stanzas of a very long poem.

4 *Ceres:* Roman goddess of the harvest.
20 *Boccaccio:* fourteenth-century Italian poet, author of *the Decameron.*
29 *Tyrian:* purple.
41 *Iris:* the rainbow.

p. 51   The Two Peacocks of Bedfont

68 *Dagon:* a heathen god of the Philistines.
124-5 *Slippers . . . satin:* the irreverent thoughts of youth are straying from religious instruction to the vanity of fine clothes.

p. 60   Sonnet: To an Enthusiast
In this address to a young idealist who has retained his idealism beyond youth, Hood expresses the conviction that he will have more than the common share of both sorrow and joy.

p. 62   Sonnet to Vauxhall
Vauxhall was an expensive pleasure garden in London. The poem describes, in a very impressionistic way, the crowds in the rain, the often pretentious conversation, the rich clothes and the fireworks of a typical evening there.

p. 63   A Drop of Gin
A sophisticated parody of a Temperance ballad.

13 *Alembic:* a chemical still or retort.
17-18 *Barebones nor Prynne:* seventeenth-century puritans.
50 *Mynn:* a famous cricketer of the period.
60 *cognovits:* acknowledgements by defendants that the plaintiff's claim is just, and his consent that judgement be entered accordingly.
64 *'louping over a linn':* hanging over a linden tree, i.e. a gallows.

p. 69   The Bridge of Sighs

10 *cerements:* shrouds.

p. 74 Stanzas

This complicated poem expresses the guilt and pain of a man falling out of love with a woman in whom he has intentionally inspired love. He finds it difficult to leave her because of his feelings of pity.

p. 75 Ode on a Distant Prospect of Clapham Academy

The footnote is, of course, ironic and is designed to point out the fact that this is a parody of Gray's *Ode on a Distant Prospect of Eton College*.

10 *iron rod:* a lightning conductor. Lightning turned the beer sour.
26 *Pallas:* Pallas Athene, the Greek goddess of wisdom.
28 *Crichton:* the original 'admirable Crichton'—whose name is now applied to any scholar—was a brilliant Scot of the sixteenth century.
30 *bohea:* tea.
37–42 References to Hood's contemporaries.
44 *'the Greys':* a regiment.
50 *Owhyee:* a not unpointed reference to the Victorian passion for missionary work.
65 *Mac-Adamized:* made smooth, with a possible reference to the blackness of tar-MacAdam.
81 *taw:* a marble.
88–90 A parody of Gray's closing lines:

> No more; where ignorance is bliss,
> 'Tis folly to be wise.

p. 79 Bailey Ballad

In a note to this poem Hood denies that the title refers to the popular contemporary writer of sentimental ballads such as 'She wore a wreath of roses', but no doubt this denial was disingenuous since his poem is an excellent parody of Haynes Bayley's manner. Hood says his title refers to the Old Bailey where he was obliged to waste long hours doing jury service.

p. 80 Mary's Ghost

19 *Mary-bone:* dialect form of Marylebone, a district of London.
20 *boned:* slang for stolen.

22 *Dr. Vyse:* the names throughout this poem are those of fictitious eminent surgeons.

p. 82   Faithless Nelly Gray

15 *pay her his devours:* to court.
36 *Badajo's breaches:* a reference to a campaign in the Peninsular War.
68 *With a stake in his inside:* to show he was a suicide.

THOMAS LOVELL BEDDOES

LIFE

Thomas Lovell Beddoes was born in 1803 into a family with both scientific and literary gifts. His mother was a sister of the novelist Maria Edgeworth, and his father, Dr Thomas Beddoes, was a well-known physician. Dr Beddoes was by all accounts a remarkable man, radical in his opinions, independent to the point of eccentricity. He was progressive and a humanitarian in the best sense. He knew and treated Coleridge and Southey among a number of eminent men. Dr Beddoes died on Christmas Eve 1808, while his son was still an infant.

The poet's sense of justice and intellectual curiosity were clearly inherited from his father. Nevertheless, his mother was an imaginative and affectionate woman, and he passed a happy enough childhood in Clifton, where he was born, and in Bath, where Mrs Beddoes moved in 1712. This was varied by visits to Maria Edgeworth's father in Ireland and in Shropshire. In 1817 Beddoes went to Charterhouse, where he had a distinguished scholastic career, which he succeeded in combining with a taste for high-spirited practical jokes. He won general respect, and his influence on his fellow-pupils was considerable. He was the inventor of a variety of slang which survived at Charterhouse for many years after his departure. His precocious imagination found rather more orthodox outlet in a keen interest in the drama: Beddoes wrote both poetry and plays, which were as full of morbid horrors as his later work was to be. In 1822, his freshman year at Pembroke, Oxford, he published *The Improvisatore*, a poetic sequence of three 'fyttes', which he dedicated to his mother 'as a slight token of her son's respect and affection'. This was followed in 1822 by *The Bride's Tragedy*, an extravagant and powerful drama which was received with great critical enthusiasm— Darley, writing in 1823 in the *London Magazine*, under the pseudonym of John Lacy, hailed Beddoes as 'a scion worthy of the stock from which Shakespeare and Marlowe sprang'. At the age of twenty, while still an undergraduate, he found himself the author of the *succès d'estime* of London literary society.

Beddoes seems to have been an unconventional and rebellious student, although little is known of his Oxford days. He did not come up at all for his first Michaelmas term, and he interrupted his B.A. examination in 1824 in order to journey to Florence, where his mother was gravely ill. When he arrived, she was dead. Beddoes was deeply affected, and from this time on his fascination with death begins to take on pathological dimensions. He had lost his closest human contact, and his youthful high spirits were increasingly subdued to a self-destructive melancholy. Nevertheless, he succeeded in taking his B.A. in 1825, and in July of that year he matriculated at the University of Göttingen, where he intended to follow his father in taking up the study of medicine.

Until this time Beddoes' life had been one of almost unbroken success. Although he had not followed up *The Bride's Tragedy* with any further publication, he was still a very young man, and must have seemed to the world, if not to himself, to be full of promise. However, a brief résumé of his wanderings from 1825 until his suicide in 1849 will reveal his isolation and the extent to which he had lost his hold on life. Not long after his arrival in Göttingen he took to heavy drinking and in 1829—following his first suicide attempt—he was sent down from the University for drunk and disorderly behaviour. He departed from the town, leaving considerable debts behind him and travelled to Würzburg, where he was admitted to the University. His friend Reich was also a student there at this time, but his name mysteriously disappears from the records only one term after Beddoes' arrival.

In the autumn of 1831 the poet became deeply involved in German radical politics, and this led to his expulsion from Würzburg the following summer. He travelled to Zürich, where he spent perhaps the five happiest years of his adult life. In 1837 he tried in vain to find a publisher for a collection of prose and verse, the fruits of his relatively settled life in Switzerland. He was also occupied in the revision of *Death's Jest Book*, the constant, and indeed obsessive, activity of all these years abroad. In 1840 his political activity again led to his expulsion, and from this time on he led a wandering, rootless life. He returned to England for a while, on his first long visit since 1825; but he found English society repugnant, and did not look up any of his old friends. In 1843 he was back in Zürich; in 1844 in Frankfurt he met Konrad Degen, an actor, his last close friend. In 1846 he returned to England, and this time saw all his remaining acquaintances; but his erratic behaviour shocked them and scandalized polite society in general. He went back to Frankfurt, where he lived the life of a beggar, tramping among the common people. Konrad Degen was the only person with whom he was in any kind of emotional contact.

Beddoes was admitted to Basle hospital in 1848, having tried to commit suicide by cutting open a leg artery. The wound became infected, and the limb had to be amputated. Although his letters to his sister in England at this time maintain a calm conversational tone—he explained to her that he was in hospital as the result of a fall from a horse—he was resolved to die, and in 1849 he at last succeeded in killing himself by means of an unidentified poison. *Death's Jest Book, or The Fool's Tragedy* was published anonymously the following year.

Beddoes' unhappy life has naturally given rise to psychological speculation. To some extent his intense morbid tendency of mind reflects the literary preoccupations of the time, and it was no doubt accentuated by his decision to live in Germany, where, as John Heath-Stubbs writes, the 'longing for extinction itself . . . seems . . . to have penetrated deeply into the communal consciousness'. But Heath-Stubbs sees a more specifically individual factor in the probable homosexuality of Beddoes. In his view the poet's awareness of his own sexual 'deviance' aroused in him a deep distaste for physical existence, which was expressed in an overpowering fascination with death and the destruction of the body.

Whatever its true cause may have been, it is certain that Beddoes' complex attitude to his own existence, and to life and death in general, is best defined in the combination of Gothic horror and gallows humour which characterizes his poetry. The note which was found by his dead body shows him in three of his various moods. First, he is self-disgusted; then for a moment aware of what he might have become; but his final comment, referring to his amputated leg, shows him taking a last refuge in ironic detachment:

I am food for what I am good for—worms . . .
I ought to have been among other things a good poet; Life was too great a bore on one peg and that a bad one.

Beddoes was a poet who, like Darley, spent much thought and energy in the cultivation of a talent for drama which he did not possess. He had no sense of construction and no psychology. But he was intensely, almost morbidly, fascinated by the obsession with death in its grimmer aspects which characterized Jacobean tragedy. Like Webster, he was 'much possessed by death', and this was a personal as well as a literary obsession on Beddoes' part. Before considering him as what he essentially was, a lyric poet with a remarkable ear and imagination, it would be well, since the drama was with him a lifelong preoccupation, to quote one typical example of his dramatic blank verse. Here are the lines in *Death's Jest Book* spoken by Wolfram immediately before the song 'Old Adam, the carrion crow'.

> Good melody! if this be a good melody,
> I have at home, fattening in my stye,
> A sow that grunts above the nightingale.
> Why this will serve for those who feeds their veins
> With crust, and cheese of dandelion's milk,
> And the pure Rhine. When I am sick o'mornings,
> With a horn-spoon tinkling my porridge-pot,
> 'Tis a brave ballad: but in Bacchanal night,
> O'er wine, red, black, or purple-bubbling wine,
> That takes a man by the brain and whirls him round,
> By Bacchus' lip I like a full-voiced fellow,
> A craggy-throated, fat-cheeked trumpeter,
> A barker, a moon-howler, who could sing
> Thus, as I heard the snaky mermaids sing
> In Phlegethon, that hydrophobic river,
> One May-morning in Hell.

This kind of writing, literary and artificial as it is, and making no contribution to the action, had no place on the stage and no future except in the historical narrative verse of Browning, who was much influenced by it.

From the first, Beddoes maintained a slender reputation as a poets' poet. He was greatly admired by Browning, who noticed his interest in the grotesque and comic elements in Jacobean drama. Shortly after Beddoes' death Henry Crabb Robinson, a discerning reader and a friend of poets, noted in his diary: 'I read with great admiration rather than pleasure Beddoes' tragedy—the first three acts of *The Fool's Tragedy* . . . [alternative title of *Death's Jest Book*] . . . I have since read the rest of this beautiful tragedy. It has marvellous power, and as the work of a young man, raises deep regret at his early death. It is replete with horror, with a grotesque combination with comedy, and also delicious songs. It deals in the supernatural and is exuberant with imagery and excessive passion.'

Arthur Symons, in the nineties, was interested in Beddoes, whom he called 'a monumental failure, more interesting than many facile triumphs'. Symons commented also on his 'strange choiceness and curiosity of phrase'. In our own century Lytton Strachey praised Beddoes, remarking that he was literary 'in the best sense', that is, in the sense in which Spenser and Milton were literary. Edmund Blunden wrote of Beddoes implying that his life never got into his verse: not directly perhaps, but it is a reflection, though an oblique one, of his inner consciousness—a consciousness in which his own sense of failure and his persistent death-wish played a large part.

David Daiches has pointed out that both Beddoes and Darley made interesting contributions to English metrics and describes his work as 'Jacobean macabre seen through eighteenth-century Gothic eyes'.

Beddoes has been called the most German of English poets, and this is very apparent in his concern with death, horror and the Gothic. His poems remind us of the etchings of Dürer, such as that of the 'Four Horsemen of the Apocalypse'. Beddoes' own experience as a medical student fostered his interest in human anatomy: 'He saw the skull beneath the skin'—indeed, outside the skin this grisly object is a constant image in his poems. When Ian Jack says: 'He remains the most tantalising of all our writers: a man of genius who wrote nothing that is commonly remembered', he is only saying, in other terms, that Beddoes is a poets' poet—one who lacks the popular appeal of his more easily memorized contemporaries: we can readily admit that he wrote no *Charge of the Light Brigade* or *Village Blacksmith*.

As with Darley it is left to John Heath-Stubbs to make the most penetrating criticism of Beddoes. He sees him as an exile to Germany from Victorian England, where he could find no place. He regards Beddoes as potentially the best of the trio of poets of which the other two were Darley and Hood. Heath-Stubbs is right to deprecate the use of the convenient label which was once attached to Beddoes—'the last Elizabethan'—for he was a true child of his own century, though his work was not in the main stream, or even one of the tributary streams. Commenting on the harshness of the imagery in much of Beddoes' work, Heath-Stubbs points out that, in many of his lyrics about death, there is something of sensuality in the imagery—

even of sexuality; he connects this with Beddoes' latent homosexuality.

As a poet, Beddoes seems not to have been interested in everyday life, from the cares and stresses of which he used poetry as a means of escape. In this he resembles Keats, who, of course, grappled with the problems of real life in a more convinced and conscious manner. The first poem in this selection, the long verse-narrative *Pygmalion*, is very reminiscent of Keats, and recalls verse-narratives on mythological subjects such as *Endymion*. Beddoes may not have dealt with the problems of real life in his poems, but he was aware of those of poetry. In the *Letter to B. W. Procter* (who achieved considerable popularity under the pseudonym of 'Barry Cornwall') he urges his fellow-poet to give up writing verse of the early Victorian tea-table kind and write something worthy and elevating, as distinct from his own jesting with death. This suggests that Beddoes was aware, not only of the shortcomings of popular contemporary verse, but of his own limitations and the narrowness of his range. His interest in intricate stanza forms and his obsession with death are illustrated everywhere in the other poems. In *The Ghosts' Moonshine* the image of a murderer's ghost blowing through a dead man's ribs is characteristic of his use of the Gothic. The *Dirge* ('If thou wilt ease thine heart') is a good example of a feature noticed by Heath-Stubbs, the sensual concern with death, the expression of a deeply felt death-wish. The *Song* ('Squats on a toadstool') is a good example of Beddoes' love of the grotesque, the bizarre and the macabre. The *Song* ('A cypress-bough, and a rose-wreath sweet') unites the two themes of marriage and death—'Death and Hymen', as he calls it. *Dream-Pedlary* and the unfinished *Lines Written in Switzerland* sound a more personal note, the latter speaking more directly than usual of Beddoes' sense of the decline of poetry in England during his life-time, of the commercialization of Britain and the fact of his own alienation from the Victorian reading public.

Beddoes, this most German of English poets, will never be popular; but if we accept the narrow range of his interests and imagery, his concern with the bizarre, his obsession with death, he remains as a reminder that under the surface of Victorian respectability, with which the received poets had to come to terms, there was another voice—the voice of rejection and alienation, an alienation made poignant by the facts of Beddoes' personal tragedy. At the heart of his failure there is a real success: through bitter experience he learned, as some 'greater' poets did not, to accept the limitations of his own nature in the context of his time and to face honestly the fact of his own defeat.

p. 86 Pygmalion

The poem presents in mythical form what Beddoes sees as the predicament of the artist: he is exclusive and a lonely searcher, yet inspired by some inner, universal force (lines 40–74). To bring about his greatest feat, creating actual life, he needs some strange material (lines 75–97). Then begins the long period of dedicated creativity. The cost of immortality is his own existence, Pygmalion dies creating life.

76 *Olympus:* mountain and home of the gods in Greek mythology.
82 *agued:* diseased.
135 *Jove:* chief of the Roman gods.
214 *Charon:* the boatman who conveyed departed souls into hell.

p. 93 Letter to B. W. Procter

6 *antediluvially:* before the flood.
20 *Circe:* the enchantress of the Odyssey.
21 *Pierian:* belonging to the Muses.
24 *Parnassus:* mountain and home of the nine muses.
39 *Jaggernaut:* from Hindu mythology—a god to whom devotees blindly sacrificed themselves.
59 *Augustus:* emperor of Rome at the time of its cultural height.
63 *Adrian:* the emperor Hadrian; *More:* St Thomas More.
65 *uncypress:* the cypress is a symbol of death.
67 *Momus:* the personification of fault-finding.
73 *Anatomy:* Burton's *Anatomy of Melancholy.*

p. 98 Song: Squats on a toad-stool

22 *Ringwood:* ale brewed at Ringwood in Hampshire.
26 *Lucifer:* the devil.

p. 99 A cypress-bough, and a rose-wreath sweet

9 *Hymen:* god of marriage.

12 *Tritons:* sea gods.

18 *orchis:* orchid.

Silenus was an aged follower of Dionysus, the Greek god of wine. He is usually represented as riding on a donkey, whose death he laments here. Proteus was an old man of the sea with the power to change his shape. In the poem Beddoes is concerned with the inevitability of life changing and leading to death.

2 *thyrsus:* a staff twined with ivy and vine leaves carried at a festival of Dionysus.
3 *Bacchantes:* female followers of Bacchus, another name for the god of wine.
8 *Ariadne:* wedded to Dionysus after her desertion by Theseus.
12 *dapple:* the name of Sancho Panza's donkey in *Don Quixote.*
13 *Elysian meadow:* a field on the Islands of the Blessed, the paradise where departed souls were said to live.
19 *son of Semele:* Dionysus himself.

These lines show Beddoes' bitterness at the unfavourable climate for poetry that existed in England at this time.

3 *roundelay:* song.
9 *Adonais:* Shelley's name for Keats in his elegy for him of that name.
17–18 Reference to Wordsworth who lived near Mount Rydal in the Lake District and who was now past his poetic best.
19 *Orion:* a hunter in Greek mythology and lover of Eos, the Dawn.
27 *Ocean-Avernus:* a coinage meaning a place of descent into hell beside the sea.
31 Britannia.

EMILY BRONTË

Emily Jane Brontë, the fifth of six children, was born in August 1818, the daughter of a clergyman. Within two years the family moved to Haworth, in Yorkshire, where Mr Brontë had taken up the curacy. Haworth was for all the sisters, but above all for Emily, the centre of their lives; it was a remote district, backward in many respects, but Emily grew so attached to its rugged beauty that she was always deeply unhappy when education or employment took her elsewhere. Since they had very few outside contacts, the life of the young Brontës revolved almost exclusively around the family. Although the children were extremely close, their childhood was not really a happy one, for they had little contact with their parents. Mrs Brontë died of cancer when Emily was only three, and the household was managed thereafter by her elder sister, Miss Branwell, a solitary, reserved woman. Mr Brontë too was remote, eating his meals alone and rarely displaying any emotion. It is said that he fed the children on potatoes without meat in order to make them tough, and that he burned a silk dress of their mother's because he thought it unduly fine.

Consumption killed Maria and Elizabeth, the two eldest children, within six weeks of one another in 1825. Soon after this Charlotte and Emily were removed from Cowans Bridge School, near Leeds, where all four children had been studying. The rest of their childhood was spent at Haworth, where they may have received some formal education at the local grammar school, and where they were free to wander on the moors, to exchange ideas and imaginings, to read in their father's library and to write.

When Emily was thirteen or fourteen she and her younger sister Anne began to create the imaginary world of Gondal, and to compose the elaborately interwoven history of its people, which occupied Emily until the end of her life. The importance of Gondal in Emily's creative development is fundamental. Although the story itself is lost, it is indisputably the source of the majority of her poems. It has been argued that it is also the basis of her great novel, *Wuthering Heights*. It is important to realize that there was nothing childish about the Gondal story; it was only begun in adolescence, and was continued throughout Emily's adult life. Cut off as she was from the emotional outlets of normal social life, it is hardly surprising that Emily's feelings demanded some form of expression. Some critics deprecate a subjective interpretation of the poems, but the fact that Gondal was a product of Emily's imagination, although it must deter us from looking to the poetry for literal biographical fact, surely need not prevent us from seeing in it the full expression of Emily's buried emotional and spiritual experience. It might fairly be said that for Emily Gondal was a reality greater than reality.

This imagined drama occupied its author during many otherwise uneventful years. She left Haworth briefly in 1835 and again in 1836; in February 1842 she went with Charlotte to work under M. Héger (the original of Paul Emmanuel in Charlotte's *Villette*) in his school in Brussels. The death of their aunt, Miss Branwell, brought the sisters back to Haworth in the autumn, and when Charlotte returned to the Continent, Emily stayed in Yorkshire, where she remained for the rest of her life.

In 1846 some of Emily's poems were included in a collection of verse written by the three sisters and published under the pseudonyms of Currer, Ellis and Acton Bell. The volume received little attention, but Emily was indifferent to its fate; she had in the first place been reluctant to include her poems, and only consented after much pressure from Charlotte, who wrote in her 'biographical notice of Ellis and Acton Bell' (1850):

> The fixed conviction I held, and hold, of the worth of these [Emily's] poems has not indeed received the confirmation of much favourable criticism; but I must retain it notwithstanding.

The following year saw the publication of *Wuthering Heights*; but soon after this events took on a darker tone. Branwell Brontë, the only son, had for some years been a source of anxiety to his father and sisters—he took opium, he drank heavily and he had attempted to seduce the wife of one of his employers. Although he was in many ways a terrifying companion—moody, violent, drunk whenever he could get money—Emily was very close to him. It has even been suggested that he wrote a good deal of *Wuthering Heights*; and although no evidence supports this view, both Emily and her sisters were much saddened by his disgrace and his failing health. He died in September 1848; at the moment of his death he struggled to his feet, fulfilling an earlier boast that he would die standing, to prove the strength of his will.

That same will power was evident in Emily's reaction to her own illness, which followed swiftly upon Branwell's death. She refused even to see a doctor until the very end. Charlotte wrote of how, 'while full of ruth for others, on herself she had no pity; the spirit was inexorable to the flesh; from the trembling hand, the unnerved limbs, the faded eyes, the same service was exacted as they had rendered in health'. She died on 19 December 1848 at the age of thirty.

The strength she showed in her suffering was the foundation of her creative power. The poem *Oh thy bright eyes must answer now* shows that her choice of solitude and endurance was the deliberate choice of an artist; her 'God of Visions' alone had the power to explain:

> Why I have persevered to shun
> The common paths that others run.

Charlotte Brontë, a dissimilar character in many respects, but often a true judge of Emily's greatness, said of her:

> I have never seen her parallel in anything. Stronger than a man, simpler than a child, her nature stood alone.

POETRY

It is not easy to praise the poems of Emily Brontë without reservations; on the other hand, it is not possible to dismiss them as in any way typical minor Victorian verse. This is because of a Blake-like intensity and immediacy, a timeless concern with life and death which lifts the poems above all trivialities. Where they fail, they fail finely; where they succeed, as in a few instances they do, they succeed magnificently and uniquely.

The faults are easy to enumerate: they occur wherever we feel that the demonic possession which inspires her best work is absent. The vocabulary is occasionally the over-lush vocabulary of early Victorian album verse. The rhythm is sometimes flat and mechanical, like that of a bad hymn. On the other hand, where the poet is deeply committed, there is no weakness, either of imagery or rhythm. She is almost at her best in evoking the bare, cold landscape of her native Yorkshire; she is a painter of sure and firm observation, in a scene where sky and moor are one in a vast, empty panorama; she does not elaborate; she paints broadly and selectively.

No discussion of Emily Brontë's poems can avoid the problem of Gondal, the setting for the imaginative Gothic saga which occupied Emily and her sisters from childhood on. The prose parts of the saga are lost, but it appears to be a Gothic romance of considerable starkness and power. What has survived is the poems, mostly short, which were interspersed in the prose. Some critical effort has been spent in showing that the poems can only be interpreted in the Gondal setting, that they were 'not personal but imaginative'—whatever that distinction may mean. I cannot accept this view, for at their best the poems sound, not like dramatic interludes, but like the confessional utterances of a highly wrought and, in the strictly human sense, deeply committed sensibility. It should be remembered that Emily Brontë was extremely reticent and shrank from all personal publicity. She and her sisters adopted masculine pseudonyms.

All the poems in this selection, except a handful, are 'Gondal' poems, and through them the personality of Emily Brontë, transmuted by her poetic medium, can be felt. Whatever relation the poems may originally have had to their narrative setting, they must be read as lyrics of individual personal feeling. They reveal a profoundly hurt nature, deprived of comfort and consolation, constrained to brood on death in stoical despair and to seek a haven in religious reassurance.

Emily Brontë was not a conspicuously accomplished technician. Too often her limited imagic and rhythmic resources fail her. In her best poems, however, such as *Remembrance*, it is irrelevant to speak of poetic technique; the utterance is inspired, the direct expression of a powerful mind charged with overmastering emotion. The intensity of the experience gives the diction and movement a strength which enables it to transcend the limits of anything that can be called ordinary Victorian lyricism. The most famous of the poems was for long *No coward soul is mine*; although there is a rhetorical note which is slightly alien to Emily Brontë's writing at its finest, we feel that the direct expression of a defiant fortitude in the face of despair is genuine, natural and inspired. If the poems relegate her to the status of minor poet, *Wuthering Heights* raises her to that of a major writer.

NOTES ON THE POEMS OF EMILY BRONTE

p. 116   To a Wreath of Snow

10 *talisman:* token, pledge.

p. 118   Lines: The soft unclouded blue of air
This is one of the Gondal poems 'probably pertaining to Douglas, suggestive of Heathcliff in *Wuthering Heights*' (Hatfield).

p. 120   And now the house-dog stretched once more
See note on previous poem, which applies also to this.

46 *basilisk:* mythological reptilian creature able to kill a victim by looking at it.

p. 121   *Sleep not, dream not*

9 *Boy:* a character in the Gondal legend.

p. 126   And like myself lone, wholly lone
The subject of this poem is a caged bird.

p. 129   O thy bright eyes must answer now
The poet here makes a deliberate choice of the life of the spirit, involving loneliness and pain, rather than the life of the world, which reason advocates, renouncing wealth, power, glory and pleasure.

33 *real:* another version has 'earthly', which is evidently the meaning.

p. 132   Death, that struck when I was most confiding
This is a puzzling poem. Obviously the feeling is genuine, profound and even passionate: there have been two emotional experiences, of which the first was blighted by a sense of guilt, and the second, innocent and even more joyful, has ended in a death. The poet now begs for a further death, evidently her own, in order that she may achieve a spiritual communion with eternity. It is when we come to examine the imagery and its inter-connections more closely that difficulties begin. I find it impossible to relate the 'tree' images with whatever actual experience underlies the poem. To regard the tree as symbolic of the poet's life in time seems to make the best sense, but this still leaves considerable confusion.

INDEX OF TITLES AND FIRST LINES

169